Rupert Isaacson

Cadogan Books plc
London House, Parkgate Road,
London SW11 4NQ, UK
Distributed in the USA by
The Globe Pequot Press
6 Business Park Road, PO Box 833, Old Saybrook,
Connecticut 06475–0833

Book and cover design by Animage
Maps © Cadogan Guides, drawn by
Map Creation Ltd
Series Editors: Rachel Fielding and Vicki Ingle
Editing: Vicki Ingle, Dominique Shead, Katrina Burroughs
Proofreading: Julie Shaw
Indexing: Dorothy Frame
Production: Rupert Wheeler Book Production Services

A catalogue record for this book is available from the British Library
ISBN 1–86011–006–1

Output by Bookworm, Manchester.
Printed and bound in the UK by Redwood Books, Trowbridge, Wilts.

The author and publishers have made every effort to ensure the accuracy of the information in the book at the time of going to press. However, they cannot accept any responsibility for any loss, injury or inconvenience resulting from the use of information contained in this guide.

Please help us keep this guide up to date

Although the information in this guide was correct at the time of printing, practical details such as opening hours, travel information, standards in hotels and restaurants and, in particular, prices are liable to change.

We would be delighted to receive any comments concerning exisiting entries or omissions. Significant contributions will be acknowledged in the next edition, and authors of the best letters will receive a copy of the Cadogan Guide of their choice.

About the Author

Rupert Isaacson has travelled extensively, feature-writing on Eastern Europe, North America, Africa and now India. He is the author of the Cadogan Guides to South India and South Africa. His mother, Polly Loxton, illustrated the guide.

Acknowledgements

First of all, thanks to Ranjan Abraham and Varkey Kurian for putting up with me, for their endless patience in securing the permission to enter the tribal areas and for proving such excellent trekking companions. Thanks also to Roma Satara for fixing my first itinerary, for looking after me long-distance in bad old Bombay and for sorting out my endless money hassles.

To Keith at Jungle Hut—thanks for showing me the trekking route up into the Nilgiris; to Mr and Mrs Kothavala at Bamboo Banks—many thanks for the Christmas dinner and good conversation; to Mahesh at Monarch Safari Camp—thank you, thank you for letting me ride your superb horses; to Yvonne and Ken Neale, thank you for the lift from Jungle Trails and for the tea that hot afternoon during Holi. And to Sini at Ooty—without you I would never have stayed with the Todas.

Dr Javarlial Rodrigues—thanks for mending me in Goa, despite my stupidity in falling off the ravine, and also to the Mallya Hospital in Bangalore for dealing with my subsequent complications at such short notice.

On the home front, thanks to Vicki for commissioning me and for all her hard work, to Justine for her superhuman ability to pull me out of the poo despite intervening oceans and time zones. To Dom and Toby thanks for pulling the book into order, to Polly, my mum, once again your pictures surpass any expectations I may have had. Vikram—I must owe you about 5000 pints, not to mention the Loony Tunes and incisive history comments. And Rachel—as always full of wisdom, sympathy and support.

Lastly Kristin, thank God you said 'yes' to Bangalore.

Contents

Religion 43–8

Architecture 49–52

Topics 53–60

Panjim and Old Goa 61–70

North Goa 71–90

South Goa 91–116

Goa's Wildlife Sanctuaries 117–20

The Karnataka and Kerala Beaches 121–31

Index 132–6

Maps

Introduction

Since its discovery by hippie travellers back in the sixties, Goa has gradually developed into one of the world's most beautiful and most affordable places to take a holiday. Yet the word 'developed' is misleading. As yet, apart from a few small resort hotels, Goa's 60-mile coastline of palm-fringed, sandy beaches remains more or less as God made it. There are no high-rise hotels, few roads even, and although some of the beaches have now become very Westernized in terms of accommodation, food and hygiene, you can still find coves and beaches where your only company will be the occasional fisherman. Whether you want luxury or just a room or cottage to stash your gear, whether you want to party yourself blind or find solitude in nature, Goa can accommodate you.

The place has its own style, distinct from the rest of India: its Portuguese and Indian cultures have produced a sub-tropical blend of Asia and the Mediterranean. Indigenous Konkani fishermen leave their long hardwood boats to worship at the white-fronted Baroque churches that seem to peep up over the palms wherever you look. Grand colonial houses share space in the villages with huts made of palm-thatch. The seafood can be curried, as in India, or cooked in wine, European-style. Behind the beaches, groves of cashew trees planted by the first Portuguese settlers give way to a distinctively Asian landscape of rice paddies.

A week or two drifting up and down the coast is heaven, but Goa has more than just beaches. Within half an hour of Panjim, the capital, there is Old Goa, one of the most dramatic collections of

Renaissance cathedral architecture in the world. Up in the mountains that run down the state's eastern border great forests are still home to elephant, bison, leopard, deer and even the occasional tiger, which you can see in wildlife sanctuaries. There are ruined Portuguese and Islamic forts, Hindu temples and ancient Buddhist sanctuaries carved into remote cliffsides. In November and December tens of thousands of migratory birds flock to the Mandovi and Zuari estuaries, turning the mangroved banks into a shifting, squawking mass of colour.

Above all, Goa is a place to relax; as well as being a holiday destination in itself, travellers on their way around India often use Goa as a place to 'escape' from the fatigues and frustrations of the rest of the sub-continent. Most of them come for a week or two and end up staying for a month or more. But it doesn't matter why you come, nor how long you stay: after your first day rocking in the warm ocean and your first night marvelling at the silver wash of moonlight turning the sand and the palm trees to liquid silver, you'll know one thing—that you want to come back.

The Best of Goa

Best Beaches: Arambol and Terekol, Betul, Benaulim, Rajabag (for peace and quiet); Anjuna and Vagator (for parties); Arambol, Terekol, Anjuna, Vagator, Benaulim, Cavelossim and Palolem (for budget travellers); Fort Aguada, Dona Paula, Bogmalo, Varca and Mabor (for expensive resorts).

Best Bars and Restaurants: The Crosshill Bar and the White House, Dona Paula; the Riverdeck and the Panjim Inn, Panjim; Grandpa's, Anjuna; Casa Portuguesa, Baga; the Haystack, Mapusa; Sousa Lobo, Calangute; 21 Coconuts, Candolim; Longuino's, Margao; The Sun and Moon, Palolem.

Best Places to Stay: Fort Aguada and Dona Paula Resorts; Nani's and Rani's, Baga; Terekol Fort; Resorte de Goa, Varca; The Bougainvillaea, Anjuna; The Panjim Inn, Panjim; Brito's Tourist Corner, Benaulim; the Guest House, Betul.

Best Historical Sites: Old Goa, Loutolim, Chandor, Rachol, Ponda, Tamdi Surla, Terekol Fort, Cabo de Rama Fort.

Best Shopping: Anjuna and Mapusa markets, Margao main market.

Best Nature: Bondla and Bhagwan Mahavir Wildlife Sanctuaries, Lake Karmali Bird Sanctuary.

Travel

Getting There

By Air

Unless you are planning to stay for less than a month and can therefore take a charter flight, you will have to fly to Goa via Bombay and travel on by domestic flight, bus or catamaran (*see* below).

The price of air tickets to India varies according to three major factors: whether you pay a full (standard) fare or a discount fare; when you go and how long you're planning to stay. If you contact an airline direct they will usually give you full fare prices, which tend to be much the same no matter what the airline. Standard fares are cheapest when you book an *excursion fare*, which requires that you stay in India for a minimum of 2 weeks and no more than 3–4 months.

Ticket prices for excursion fares vary according to whether it is high season (July–August and December–January) or low season (anytime outside the above dates).

From the UK

standard carriers

It should be stressed that this is *not* the most economical way to go and that prices become vastly reduced if you go through the discount travel agents listed below. Also, none of the standard carriers fly direct to Goa; you have to fly first to Bombay and then take an onward flight, which makes the cost very high. To avoid this, either fly direct to Goa on a charter flight (also listed below), which allows a stay of up to one month, or on a discount flight to Bombay and then on to Goa by domestic flight, bus, train or catamaran (*see* p.8).

The British Airways standard round-trip excursion fare from London (low season, economy class, 4-month stay) is £1524 to Goa and £700 to Bombay, bookable one month in advance. In high season the fare remains at £1524 for Goa and goes up to £770 for Bombay. Airlines providing good, regular and reliable services from the UK to India include **Air India**, **British Airways**, **Air France**, **Cathay Pacific**, **Emirates**, **Gulf Air**, **KLM**, **JAL**, **Lufthansa**, **Thai International**, **Alitalia**, **Swissair**, and **Singapore Airlines**. Students under 26 should enquire about the generous student discounts offered by some of these airlines, notably Thai International and Singapore Airlines.

discount air travel

Direct charter flights (valid for up to one month) to Goa from the United Kingdom are now offered by **British Caledonian**, **Monarch** and **Air Europe**. The average low season price for these tickets is between £280 and £330, while high season tickets cost approximately £380 to £440.

For stays of longer than two weeks you can book open-ended returns to Goa via Bombay through most 'bucket shop' discount travel agents. The average cost for a 12-month open-ended return to Goa from London is about £360 low season and £550–£600 in high season.

finding the cheapest fare

Many cheap bargains are advertised in magazines like *Time Out*, *LAM*, *TNT* and *Australasian Express*, and there are many cut-price travel agencies around Earl's Court, London. For example, a discounted 4-month excursion fare on Lufthansa from London to Bombay costs £385 in low season and £462 in high season. Gulf Air usually offers very cheap fares to India (you cannot buy directly from Gulf Air but must go through a travel agent). Their tickets are valid for one year and cost £468 in low season and £590 in high season to Bombay. Contact the following travel agencies for good deals on flights:

Flamingo Travel, 24 Wardour Street, London WC1, ✆ (0171) 287 0402

Flightbookers, 118 Tottenham Court Road, London WC1, ✆ (0171) 757 2000

GSA Hindustan Travel, 30 Poland Street, London WC1, ✆ (0171) 439 9801

STA Travel, 117 Euston Road, London NW1, ✆ (0171) 937 9962

Trailfinders, 42–50 Earls Court Road, London W8, ✆ (0171) 938 3366.

From the USA

The full fare from New York to Bombay on Air India (4-month maximum stay) costs US$1433 in low season, US$1601 in high season, and US$2722 for a one-year ticket.

For discounted tickets, try calling STA Travel in New York, ✆ (212) 477 7348, or San Francisco, ✆ (415) 391 8407, or look in the Sunday travel section of your nearest big city newspaper. To save money and to get the best flight availability, many American travellers fly into New York on cheap internal flights from various other parts of the country. Those flying from the west coast may also save money by flying west via Bangkok, as certain airlines—Singapore, United, Korean and Northwest Orient—offer discounted rates in this direction.

While discounts can be found in the USA if you're prepared to shop around, it is sometimes easier to get decent fare concessions in the UK. Many American visitors travel to India by booking a flight to London, where cheap flight deals are readily available, then making another booking from London to India (call the travel agencies listed in the UK section to pre-book the connecting flight from the UK to India).

From Australia and New Zealand

From **Australia**: full fare from Sydney to Bombay on Cathay Pacific (3-month maximum stay) costs A$1868 in low season, A$2322 in high season and A$4956 for a one-year ticket. From **New Zealand**: full fare from Auckland to Bombay on Cathay Pacific (3 month maximum stay) costs NZ$2150 in low season, NZ$2350 in high season and NZ$5596 for a one-year ticket. Note that this flight requires an overnight stay in Hong Kong.

Many Australian and New Zealand travellers save money by getting cheap tickets to Singapore or Bangkok and flying on to India from there. **Jetset**, 99 Walker Street, North Sydney, N.S.W., ✆ (02) 956 9333, offers attractive flight discounts or try the **STA Travel** chain in both Australia and New Zealand. Possibly the cheapest Australia/New Zealand–India option of all is a flight hop to Bali, followed by an overland trek up through Southeast Asia.

From within India

by air

Indian Airlines have at least two flights daily between Bombay and Goa, as do **Damania**, **East West** and **Modiluft**; during the peak winter months of December and January a third and occasionally a fourth daily flight are introduced. There are regular flights to Delhi, Cochin, Bangalore, Madras and Trivandrum, also from Goa's Diabolim airport. At Diabolim outside the state's one industrial town of Vasco da Gama, the major hotels have set up reception counters and many operate free transfers by coach for prospective guests. Otherwise, it's an airport bus or a Rs200, 7-mile taxi-ride along twisting country roads into the capital, Panjim.

by catamaran

In 1995 the long disused Bombay–Goa shipping service was re-opened by Damania, replacing the old boat journey of several days with a new high-speed catamaran that takes only 8 hours. Unfortunately the catamaran service costs much the same as a flight to Bombay (in 1995 approximately US$40), so there is no saving, only the fun of rushing down the coastward waters of the Malabar Coast with the hazy blue line of the Western Ghats marching forever to the east. Another problem is the potential for delays and cancellations due to poor weather conditions.

The catamaran leaves Bombay from New Ferry Wharf, Mallet Bunder. Reservations can be made from MTDC, Madame Cama Road, Nariman Point, ✆ 2026713, 10 to 3 daily except Monday. Return reservations from Bombay can be made from any Indian Tourist Office. In Goa you can make them from V.S. Dempo and Co., Custom Wharf, ✆ 3842, direct from the Damania office opposite the steamer jetty in Panjim; or from the Government of India Tourist Office in Margao.

by train

A narrow-gauge line links Goa with Miraj from where broad-gauge trains will soon run to Bangalore, Bombay and Pune (line re-opens in 1996). Trains between Bombay and Vasco da Gama (for Bogmalo beach) and Margao or 'Madgaon' (get off here for buses to Panjim) take a long 20–22 hours and are generally on hard wooden seats but are still more comfortable than the bus.

Rail bookings can be made in Panjim at the KTC Terminal, ✆ (0832) 45620, at Margao Station, ✆ (0834) 222252, and Vasco Station, ✆ (0834) 2396.

by bus

Several luxury buses, both state and private, link Bombay and Goa daily, journey time is 16–18 hours. Most of them are of the dreaded 'video' variety. The least unpleasant, by all accounts, are those operated by Maharastra State Transport Development Corporation. There's a particularly good MRSTDC bus leaving Bombay for Panjim at 3pm daily. If returning from Goa to catch a plane in Bombay, then the bus driver can deposit you at the closest point to the airport to save going all the way into Bombay centre, only to have to trek out again.

Entry Formalities

Passports and Visas

All foreign visitors to India must obtain a **visa** in advance from the Indian embassy or consulate of their home country. Make sure you have a full, up-to-date passport. Visa fees and requirements change frequently, so use the following information as a general guide only and check with your nearest Indian tourist office or consulate for exact information.

The **standard tourist visa** is valid for either 90 or 180 days and entitles the holder to multiple entries into India within that period. Visas can be applied for from any Indian consular office or High Commission. In the UK, a multiple entry visa costs £13 for 90 days or £26 for 180 days (prices vary in other nations). Once in India, visa extensions can be obtained from various Foreigners' Registration Offices. Special long-term visas are available for business, education, the study of yoga, dance, traditional medicine or other specific projects. Applications for these visas must be submitted well in advance.

Apply for visas in the **UK** to the High Commission of India, Consular Dept., India House, Aldwych, London WC2B 4NA, ✆ (0171) 836 8484/0990, 9.30am to 5.30pm. Application forms are available from the Commission office, and also from the Government of India Tourist Office, 7 Cork Street, London W1, ✆ (0171) 437 3677, @ (0171) 494 1048. You can apply either by post, which can take up to four weeks to process (send passport, three passport photos and postal order to 'High Commission of India'); or in person, which takes just 24 hours. Arrive with your passport, three passport-size photos and an application form at the High Commission building, 9am latest, to avoid the queues. It's open 9.30am to 1.00pm weekdays and you'll have to return the next working day to collect your passport and visa between 4.30 and 5.30pm.

Trailfinders, Thomas Cook and American Express have quick, efficient visa services for travellers and for a small charge will do all the waiting and queuing for you.

Travellers from other nations should apply to the Indian embassy, consulate or high commission nearest them.

Australia: 3–5 Moonah Place, Yarralumla, ACT 2600, ✆ (062) 733 999

Canada: 10 Springfield Road, Ottawa, K1M 1C9, ✆ (613) 744 3751

Ireland: 6 Lesson Park, Dublin 6, ✆ (1) 4970843

New Zealand: 180 Molesworth Street, Princess Towers, Wellington, ✆ (4) 73 6390

UK: India House, Aldwych, London WC2B 4NA, ✆ (0171) 836 8484; 82 New Street, Birmingham B2 4BA, ✆ (0121) 212 2782

USA: 2107 Massachusetts Avenue NW, Washington, DC 20008, ✆ (202) 939 7000; 3 East 64th Street, New York, NY 10021, ✆ (212) 879 7888; 540 Arguello Boulevard, San Francisco, CA 94118, ✆ (415) 668 0662

If you want to **extend your visa**, the Foreigners' Regional Registration Offices is based in **Bombay**: Annexe 2, Police Headquarters, Near Crawford Market, 400 001, ✆ 2611169

customs formalities and regulations

Visitors are required to make an oral baggage declaration upon arrival and should also fill in the Disembarkation Card given to them by the airlines during the course of their flight to India. Personal effects such as jewellery, cameras or cassette players are allowed duty free into the country. Up to 200 cigarettes and 1 litre of alcohol are also allowed duty free. It is prohibited to bring weapons, live plants and gold or silver bullion into the country.

Upon leaving India an Embarkation Card should be filled out. There are restrictions on the export of antiquities and art objects more than 100 years old and it is forbidden to take articles made from indigenous wild animals, such as skins, ivory, or rhino horns, out of the country.

foreign travel tax

All visitors are required to pay a Foreign Travel Tax of Rs300 upon departure (Rs150 if travelling on to Afghanistan, Bangladesh, Bhutan, Burma, Nepal,

Pakistan, Sri Lanka, the Andamans, Lakshadweeps or the Maldives). If flying, you pay the tax at a special desk located in all international airports, which usually accepts foreign currency if you've spent all your rupees. If travelling to islands off-shore, your travel agent will levy the tax in his or her tariff.

Main Agents and Special-interest Holidays

Main Agents and Operators

These offer general bookings for Goa and onward itineraries anywhere alse in the country. The companies in the first paragraphs of the UK and US sections are expensive, the ones in the second paragraphs moderate.

in the UK

Abercrombie & Kent, Sloane Square House, Holbein Place, London SW1 8NS, ✆ (0171) 730 9600, @ (0171) 730 9376. A&K offer expensive set tours or private itineraries, as well as specialist sporting holidays (*see* below). **Cox & Kings**, St James' Court, Buckingham Gate, London SW1E 6AF, ✆ (0171) 873 5000, @ (0171) 873 5008. **Global Link Ltd**, Colette House, 52–55 Piccadilly, London W1V 9AA, ✆ (0171) 409 7766, @ (0171) 409 0545. **Petitts India**, 14 Lonsdale Gardens, Tunbridge Wells, Kent, TN1 1NV, ✆ (01892) 515966, @ (01892) 515951.

Bales Tours, Bale House, Junction Road, Dorking, Surrey, RH4 3EJ, ✆ (01306) 885 991, @ (01306) 740 048. **Cape Travel Agency**, 28 High Street, Teddington, Middlesex, TW11 8EW, ✆ (0181) 943 4067, @ (0181) 943 4086. **Elite Vacations Ltd**, Elite House, 98–100 Besborough Road, Harrow, Middlesex, HA1 3DT, ✆ (0181) 864 4431, @ (0181) 426 9178. **Inspirations Holidays**, Victoria House, Victoria Road, Horley, Surrey, RH6 7AD, ✆ (01293) 822244, @ (01293) 821732. **Jasmine Tours Ltd**, High Street, Cookham, Maidenhead, Berks, SL6 6SQ, ✆ (016285) 31121, @ (016285) 29444. **Manos Holidays** (Kerala only), 168–172 Old Street, London EC1V 9BP, ✆ (0171) 216 8000, @ (0171) 216 8099. **Mysteries of India** (beach holidays only), 92 The Green, Southall, Middlesex, UB2 4BG, ✆ (0181) 574 2727, @ (0181) 571 0707. **NADFAS Tours**, Hermes House, 80–98 Beckenham Road, Beckenham, Kent, BR3 4RH, ✆ (0181) 658 2308, @ (0181) 658 4478. **Puma Menon Tours**, 564 Kingsbury Road, London NW9 9HJ, ✆ (0181) 204 9905, @ (0181) 206 0818. **Somak Holidays**, Somak House, Wembley Hill Road, Wembley, Middlesex, HA9 8BU, ✆ (0181) 903 8166, @ (0181) 903 9464. **Ultimate Holidays Ltd**, Twyford Business Centre, London Road, Bishop's Stortford, Herts, CM23 3YT, ✆ (01279) 508034, @ (01279) 655603.

in the USA

Abercrombie & Kent, 1520 Kensington Road, Oak Brook, IL 60521–2141, ✆ (708) 954 2944, @ (708) 954 3324. **Cox & Kings**, 511 Lexington Avenue, New York, NY 10017, ✆ (212) 935 3935, @ (212) 751 4091. **Sita World Travel Inc.**, G.M. Plaza, 767 Fifth Avenue, New York, NY 10153, ✆ (212) 759 8979, @ (212) 759 0814. **Lotus Travel**, 475 Fifth Avenue, No.1112, New York, NY 10017, ✆ (800) 998 6116.

South India Travel Agency Ltd, 352 Seventh Avenue, New York, NY 10001, ✆ (212) 631 7520, @ (212) 265 3770. **Rama Tours**, 8 South Michigan Avenue, No.20003, Chicago, IL 60603, ✆ (312) 853 3330, @ (312) 853 0225. **World Wide Travel**, 1815 H. Street NW, Suite 10001, Washington DC 20006, ✆ (202) 659 6430, @ (202) 659 1111. **Absolute Asia**, 155 W. 68th Street, Suite 525, New York, NY 10023, ✆ (800) 736 8187. **Asia Pacific Travel Ltd**, P.O. Box 350, Kenilworth, IL 60043, ✆ (800) 262 6420. **India Tours**, 230 N. Michigan Avenue, Chicago, IL 60601, ✆ (312) 726 6091, @ (312) 726 6121. **Geeta Tours and Travels**, 1245 W. Jarvis Avenue, Chicago, IL 60626, ✆ (312) 262 4978, @ (312) 262 4978.

Special-interest Holidays

For special-interest holidays in Goa, Karnataka or Kerala, book direct with a good Indian agent. Goa's only real special-interest activity is trekking in the mountains but the other two states offer a variety of options. The south's best agent for **trekking, riding, wildlife viewing** or **cultural activities** is **Clipper Holidays**, Suite 406, Regency Enclave, 4 Magrath Road, Bangalore 560 025, ✆/@ (080) 5599032/34/5599833, tlx 0845-3095. Travellers wanting to hook up with special interest activities in the north should contact **Distant Frontiers**, B2/1, Safdarjung Enclave, New Delhi 110029, ✆ (011) 6858857, @ (011) 6875553.

Getting Around

Unless you are flying (hardly necessary in Goa, but useful for getting on down the coast) travel in India is slow. Whether by bus or train you should reckon on an average of 20–25 miles per hour in flat country and 12–18 miles per hour in mountains. Even the trunk roads are seldom more than two lanes wide and are always clogged with bullock carts, trucks, cyclists, walkers or people sitting inexplicably in the path of the traffic. Trains are more comfortable than buses but no faster.

Always book your onward bus or train ticket as soon as you arrive at a place: if you decide to stay longer then losing your reservation doesn't matter but leaving your departure to the last minute always seems to coincide with a miraculous drying-up of available tickets.

By Air

Most of the air traffic inside the Indian subcontinent is handled by **Indian Airlines**, although they are increasingly being given competition by smaller, private airlines such as Damania, ModiLuft, East West and Vayudoot. Prices tend to remain constant for whichever airline.

transport to and from the airports

Once you've arrived at an airport, you normally have three options for getting into town: taxi, auto-rickshaw and bus (unless you're staying at a luxury hotel which offers a courtesy van). Taking a bus into town is the cheapest option but buses often stop running by 10pm—no use if your flight has arrived in the early hours (as international flights often do). If you are arriving late at night, the most convenient way to get into town is by pre-paid taxi (look for the pre-paid taxi counters inside the airport).

booking

Book internal air flights well in advance, as demand normally exceeds availability. Go to a travel agent to buy your ticket, as they will find you the best price and not charge any commission.

discounts

Domestic flights are surprisingly good value. Youth and student discounts from 25% to 50% are often available, so make sure you ask your travel agent if you qualify. If you have booked your flights from home you'll need to reconfirm your entire itinerary immediately to be sure of keeping your reservations.

Indian Airlines offers a 25% youth discount for those between 12 and 30 years of age. Children between 2 and 12 get a 50% discount and infants under 2 travel at 10% of the adult fare. Students between 12 and 26 years of age get a 50% student discount, though certain formalities prior to booking student tickets are required. Check with your travel agent for details.

Indian Airlines also offers air packages which function similarly to rail passes. They're not bad value if you're planning to make a lot of flights. The 'Discover India' package buys 21 days of unlimited economy class air travel anywhere in India for US$400. The 'India Wonderfares' package gets you 7 days unlimited economy class travel within one region of India (north, south, east, or west) for US$200.

Indian Airlines tickets are refundable up to one hour before scheduled flight departure, minus a Rs100 fee. No refunds are applicable for lost tickets. If your flight is delayed for over one hour, a full refund is also allowed.

Indian Airlines Offices

Bombay: Air India Building, Ist Floor, Madam Cama Road, Nariman Point, ✆ 2876161, airport, ✆ 6114433 (the airport line is open 24hrs a day).

Cochin: Durbar Hall Road, Ernakulam, ✆ 353901, airport, ✆ 364433.

Goa (Diabolim): Dempo House, Cample, Panjim, ✆ 4067, airport, ✆ 2568.

Trivandrum: Near Mascot Hotel, Museum Road, ✆ 62288, airport, ✆ 72740.

domestic flight timetable

Below is a schedule of regular flights offered by major carriers within India. The fares quoted below are Indian Airlines' one-way, full adult fares; the private airlines flying the same routes usually offer very similar fares. Scheduled flight days and fares may have changed since the time of writing.

Code: Damania Airways = DA; East West Airlines = EWA; Indian Airlines = IA; Jet Airways = JA; Modiluft = ML; NEPC Airlines = NA.

Flights available	Fare (Rs)	Airlines
Bombay to:		
Cochin (daily)	2985	IA, EWA, JA
Goa (daily)	1352	IA, DA, JA, EWA,
Mangalore (daily)	2140	IA, EWA, JA
Trivandrum (daily)	3440	IA, EWA
Cochin to:		
Bombay (daily)	2985	IA, JA, EWA, ML
Goa (daily ex Sun)	2019	IA
Trivandrum (daily ex Sun)	829	IA
Goa to:		
Bombay (daily)	1352	IA, DA, JA, EWA, ML
Cochin (daily ex Sun)	2019	IA
Trivandrum (daily ex Sun)	2428	IA
Mangalore to:		
Bombay (daily)	2140	IA, JA, EWA
Trivandrum to:		
Bangalore (Mon/Tues/Thurs/Sat)	1841	IA
Bombay (daily)	3440	IA, EWA
Cochin (daily ex Sun)	829	IA
Goa (daily ex Sun)	2428	IA

By Boat

You can travel by catamaran from Bombay to Goa and take small-boat trips through the backwaters of Kerala. The Bombay–Goa catamaran takes 8 hours and costs about US$40 for foreigners, but you get a wonderful view of the mountainous Malabar Coast and schools of dolphins play across the bows (*see* p.101 for full details).

By Rail

Within Goa there is only a light-gauge railway line linking the towns of Vasco da Gama and Margao with the mountains in the east of the state. Long-distance rail journeys to and from Goa are long and tedious, as they necessitate a change of trains (from light-gauge to heavy-gauge) at the little town of Miraj. From here, you can take onward trains to Bombay and Delhi. However, it must be said that it is far quicker to reach Bombay by bus. There is no railway linking Goa with the Karnataka or Kerala coasts but these can also be reached by bus (*see* p.122 for full details).

If your trip to Goa and the southern coast is only part of a greater trip within India, then it is worth knowing how the railways work. Buy a copy of ***Trains at a Glance***. Sold cheaply at most large rail stations, this booklet provides a complete timetable of the rail services in India.

There are five basic classes of passenger rail travel: 1st class air-conditioned sleeper (operates on certain trains and routes only); 2nd class air-conditioned sleeper; 2nd class air-conditioned chair-car; 1st class non air-conditioned and 2nd class non air-conditioned. For overnight journeys, the nicest way to travel is via 2nd class air-conditioned sleeper (costing half of the overrated 1st class air-conditioned sleeper fare, far more private and comfortable), but a 2nd class non air-conditioned sleeper is relatively clean and comfortable and is very inexpensive. Always choose the quicker mail, express or superfast trains, as local passenger trains take ages.

You should always make a reservation for air-conditioned and sleeper classes. Popular routes often fill up weeks in advance so the sooner you book your ticket the better. Train reservations are made at a separate reservation office normally adjacent to the station. If your train is full, ask for the **tourist quota** of tickets, usually issued by the District Commercial Superintendent of the railway department. His office is sometimes miles away from the station but you'll be surprised how easily he'll supply you with a ticket. Other 'quotas' are hidden away in all sorts of subterranean places in and out of the station complex.

Once you have bought a ticket your carriage and seat number will be printed on it and there will also be a 'reservation sheet' posted on the sides of each carriage which will have your name and berth number printed on it (assuming you've bought a reserved ticket).

Indian rail fares (Rs)

Note that railway tickets can be cancelled and your money fully refunded (minus a Rs10–30 cancellation fee) if you cancel more than one day in advance. You pay a 25% cancellation charge if your ticket is cancelled one day in advance up to 6 hours before scheduled departure and 50% if cancelled within 6 hours before scheduled departure and up to 3 hours after the actual departure of the train.

The following table lists railway fares on routes to the south coast originating from Bombay.

Station	*miles*	*1st a/c*	*2nd a/c*	*1st*	*a/c chair*	*2nd*
Bombay to:						
Vasco da Gama (Goa)	477	1234	698	541	310	179
Cochin (Kerala)	1148	2286	1216	1001	543	289
Trivandrum (Kerala)	1278	2475	1291	1081	581	302

Indrail Passes

If you're going to be doing a lot of rail travel the Indrail Pass can be very good value. Valid for one year from purchase date, it gives unlimited travel on Indian trains for specified lengths of time (e.g. 7 days, 60 days) and allows you to go where and when you like without ever (if travelling unreserved) having to join a ticket queue. If you do want a reservation, you'll still have to queue but the Indrail Pass carries a bit of weight and often produces quotas denied to other ordinary rail travellers. It is also very useful for gaining access to 1st class station waiting-rooms and retiring-rooms. Buy your Indrail Pass from a travel agent; payment is accepted only in US dollars or pounds sterling.

Outside India, Indrail Passes can only be bought through authorized agents. In the UK you can buy the Indrail Pass from S.D. Enterprises Limited, 103 Wembley Park Drive, Wembley, Middlesex, HA9 8HG; in France, from Carrefour, 15 Rue des Ecoles, Paris; in the USA, from Hari World Travels, 30 Rockefeller Plaza, Shop No.21, Mezzanine North, New York; and in Australia, from Penthouse Travel, Suite 5, Level 13, Commercial Union House, 109 Pitt Street, Sydney

Indrail Pass Costs (US$)

Validity	*1st a/c*	*2nd a/c, 1st, a/c chair*	*2nd class*
7 days	270	135	70
15 days	330	165	80
21 days	400	200	110
30 days	500	250	135
60 days	720	360	165
90 days	960	480	210

By Car

Driving a car yourself is more hassle than it is worth—Indian roads being sheer hell for anyone unused to them. Car hire in India is relatively new and even Hertz, Budget and EuropCar offer both self-drive cars and ones with drivers. Mad streams of crazy traffic, aimless herds of sacred cows, nippier pigs and goats and deep pot-holes make Indian driving something of an endurance test. If you want to travel by car, use taxis or hire a car *and* driver. This will secure you a chauffeur-driven Hindustan Ambassador (an unashamed replica of the mid-50s British Morris Oxford). The driver often doubles up as a trained guide, as well as useful interpreter and watchman.

hiring motorbikes

This is a standard way for getting around Goa and motobike hire is available in most places—just ask your lodge or hotel owner. Prices range from about Rs150 per day for a Honda scooter to Rs250 per day for an Enfield bullet.

Although motorbikes are great fun, the roads are dangerous and many travellers end up hurting themselves quite seriously. If you have not riden a motorbike before, start with one of the Honda scooters, which have automatic gears, and ride that until you feel you are ready to cope with something larger. If possible, persuade somebody more experienced to give you a couple of lessons before you tackle the roads solo, especially at night.

Motorbike hire on the Karnataka and Keralan coasts is harder to organize and you will have to ask at the local tourist office.

By Bus and Luxury Coach

You can get just about anywhere by bus and it's cheap. India has a very extensive and comprehensive bus system. Each state offers its own service—usually a combination of local, deluxe, super-deluxe and video buses—and tickets are usually purchased direct from the state bus stands. Buses are often cheaper than the trains and go to several places not linked by rail. They can also be a lot quicker.

Buses leave very frequently, often every hour or half-hour and they are much less trouble to book and board than trains. Buying a reservation slip often gets you onto buses where seats are likely to be at a premium, but you will need to turn up at the bus station at least 40 minutes in advance to be sure of getting one.

Local buses are incredibly cheap and will often run you from one end of a state to another for less than Rs50, but they are also crowded, occasionally smelly and usually uncomfortable. Air-conditioned 'deluxe' buses are slightly less so. Video bus journeys are a nightmare with constant disco music and blaring video show.

Whenever leaving a bus to go to the toilet or to eat, leave a newspaper or something on your seat. This will reserve it. Take any other hand luggage off the bus with you. Backpacks and large cases are usually strapped under tarpaulin on the bus roof or stored in the hold-all.

prices

A seat on a deluxe bus is approximately 2 to 3 times the price of one on an ordinary bus—but some large Europeans literally cannot *fit* into the space offered in the latter. Prices vary but it is almost always the case that they will be a fraction lower than the fare for a 2nd class rail ticket along the same route. The longer the journey, the lower the rate per mile.

By Taxi and Auto-rickshaw

These are the two most common forms of in-town transport, most popular for short-distance hops to and from bus and rail stations when loaded down with luggage or for solo sightseeing in smaller towns and villages where tour buses aren't such good value. Taxis are usually black with yellow tops, cost around Rs6–7 per mile with a minimum fare of Rs5.60 and are quite comfortable. Auto-rickshaws are three-wheeled scooters (a two-stroke motorcycle engine with two-seater canopy strapped behind it), which are noisy, less comfortable, but very nippy. They cost between Rs4 and Rs5 per mile.

Taxis and auto-rickshaws are usually metered but the meters do not often work. You're wise to fix the cost of your journey before setting off. A succession of recent fuel price increases has left taxi meter-readings way out of date. You'll often be handed a fare adjustment card indicating a far higher fare than that shown on the meter.

If overcharged—you've agreed a fair rate for the journey in advance but the driver wants more at the end of it—don't get angry. Just write down the taxi number and announce in a calm, determined voice that you're going to the police. There are stiff fines for extorting money from tourists and your driver will usually 'remember' the correct fare instantly.

If hiring a taxi or auto-rickshaw between 11pm and 5am, be prepared to pay an additional 15% (up to 25% in the big cities) on top of the usual daytime fare.

motorcycle taxis

This is probably the most convenient way of getting around the countryside in Goa, especially between beaches or villages, and it is cheaper than either a taxi or an auto-rickshaw (usually about Rs10 per person per 10km, though you'll have to haggle). Drivers can fit up to three people onto their machines—usually large Enfield Bullets. They can also fit rucksacks and other baggage, but generally demand extra money for this. You can either wave the drivers down or find them at motorbike taxi ranks in most beach villages—usually near the village's largest hotel.

By Bicycle

In the quieter towns and beach villages, bike hire is a good option for getting around. The usual daily tariff is about Rs30 (though you may have to bargain for this) and you can get a list of hiring centres from the local tourist information office. You should *always* test the brakes, wheels (for true running and healthy spokes), look at the tyres and try the seat before you hire. Most places will let you take a trial run around the block. If they refuse, don't hire from them. Don't bother with bikes in the big cities unless you have some experience with Indian traffic—it simply isn't worth the risk. The one thing your bike *must* have is a bell. In dense traffic you'll be ringing this continually (like everybody else) to avoid being mown down. If you get a puncture you'll have no difficulty finding a repair man, they're all over the place—but you may well be hanging around for an hour while he spends overlong fixing it. Women in India travel side-saddle on cycles, so there is a great shortage of ladies' bikes. To snap up the few there are, be at the cycle-hire shop first thing in the morning.

Guided Tours

The **Government of Goa Tourism Department** offers several useful tours along the coast, up the Mandovi and Zuari estuaries and into the various inland sites (including a couple of the mountain wildlife sanctuaries). These tours operate from Panjim, Margao and sometimes from Mapusa and Colva. Most are day-tours with an average tariff per person of about Rs50–80. The few overnight tours cost about Rs250. Book via the main tourist offices in the big towns. The following is a comprehensive list of tours on offer.

North Goa Tour (leaves from Panjim, Margao and Colva) runs every day and includes the Pilar Monastary, Old Goa, Chorao Bird Sanctuary, Mayem Lake, Mapusa, Vagator, Anjuna, Calangute and Fort Aguada.

South Goa Tour (leaves from Panjim and Margao) runs every day and covers Old Goa, the Ponda Temples, Margao, Colva, Pilar Monastary, Dona Paula and Miramar.

The Traditional Tour (leaves from Panjim, Margao, Colva and Vasco da Gama by arrangement) covers Colva, the Ponda Temples, Old Goa, Pilar Monastary, Goa University (yawn), Dona Paula, Miramar and Panjim. From Panjim there is an optional evening river cruise for Rs45.

The Panjim Special (leaves from Panjim daily) covers Panjim, Old Goa and the Ponda Temples only.

The Holiday Special (leaves from Panjim daily) covers the Bondla Wildlife Sanctuary via the Ponda Temples and Tamdi Surla Temple.

The Beaches Special (leaves from Panjim daily) covers Calangute, Anjuna and Vagator and is useful for independent travellers looking for cheap accommodation.

The Island Special (leaves from Panjim daily) and covers Old Goa, Diwar Island, the Saptakoshwar Temple, Mayem Lake and the Chorao Bird Sanctuary.

The Dudhsagar Special (overnight from Panjim and Margao by arrangement). From Panjim the tour covers Old Goa, Ponda, Bondla, Tamdi Surla Temple, a night-stop at Bhagwan Mahavir Wildlife Sanctuary Resort (shared rooms) and Dudhsagar Falls in the morning, then home. From Margao, the tour covers Colva, Cortalim, Loutolim, Borim, Ponda, Bondla, Tamdi Surla, and then continues as above.

The Terekhol Fort Special (leaves from Panjim and Margao daily) involves an overnight stop at Mapusa and visits Bicholim, Anjuna, Vagator, Calangute and Fort Aguada on the way home.

The Festival Special leaves from Panjim by arrangement, and in certain seasons only, with fares based on distance. Contact Panjim Tourist Office for full details.

River Cruises leave every evening from Panjim and head out along the Mandovi estuary with stops to see 'cultural entertainments' such as Portuguese and Konkani traditional dancing and sometimes visiting an old colonial villa. The **Sunset Cruise** leaves at 6pm and lasts an hour. The **Sundown Cruise** leaves at 7.15pm and also lasts an hour. The **Full Moon Cruise** leaves at 8.30pm when there is a moon and lasts two hours. You can have dinner on board for an extra Rs80.

Practical A–Z

Climate and When to Go

The climate in Goa is most pleasant from **November to February**. It is less crowded but hot from **March to April**. Be sure to avoid **May**, the month of Indian annual holidays, when some beaches are packed with camera-clicking voyeurs. The monsoon season is from **June to October**. Temperatures usually range from 21° in November to 32°C in July and August, but it can get much hotter, of course... It is best to avoid the monsoons, when mountain trekking is not possible because of leeches and flash-floods, and the heavy rains also put a dampener on beach going.

Most foreign tourists visit Goa in season (November to February) to enjoy the best weather and facilities and to meet other travellers: Christmas is the most popular time, especially for those into the rave scene. However, a cunning minority of travellers go off season—usually a week or two before everybody else—to take advantage of the 30–50% accommodation discounts usually offered.

Communications

Post offices in India provide a good, reliable service and are open from 10am to 5pm on weekdays, until midday on Saturday. The cost of postage for letters sent within India is Rs1, and for international mail the cost is Rs11 for a letter, Rs6.50 for an aerogramme and Rs6 for a postcard. Mail sent to Europe, North America, Australia or New Zealand usually takes 10 to 14 days to reach its destination. Most of the larger post offices now offer a Speed Post service which links over 60 towns in India and delivers to most countries worldwide. For sending documents this service is a bit slower than a private courier company, but costs about half as much. For example, a speed posted letter sent from India will reach the UK in 4 to 5 days and costs Rs400. Private courier companies such as Blue Dart (the Indian company linked up with Federal Express) can deliver a letter in 2 to 3 days, but it will cost you Rs900.

A word of warning: enterprising postal staff have been known to remove unfranked (uncancelled) stamps from letters and postcards, which then go precisely nowhere. Either have your mail franked before your very eyes in a post office, or (better) buy a stack of pre-stamped aerogrammes which can't be interfered with.

Telephones tend to be unreliable, as the quality of the line often depends on the weather. The system is improving but many exchanges are overloaded and this leads to problems. With local calls you'll either get through immediately, not at all, or get connected to a number other than the one you dialled! If you don't get straight through to someone on a local call, hail a rickshaw and visit them personally, it could be much quicker. Luckily there seem to be far fewer problems with long-distance calling.

To make a long-distance call (or a local call for that matter) you can go to any number of STDs (Subscriber Trunk Dialling). These are privately run companies that offer international or interstate calling at government authorized rates. International calls cost you about Rs80 per minute, with interstate rates varying depending on distance and time of day (rates go down after 9pm). Some STDs are high-tech communications centres complete with fax machines, whereas others consist merely of a booth in a xerox shop or perhaps a phone on a shelf at a roadside food stall. It's easy to spot these centres by their large posted signs reading STD/ISD. Making calls at STDs is easy and efficient—simply make your call and a digital readout let's you know how much cash you owe to the shopkeeper. STDs are everywhere, so are extremely handy.

Fax services are available in most of the larger towns, as well as busy tourist centres such as Colva and Calangute. You can usually send a fax at a luxury hotel, though their rates are often exorbitant, or at some of the better STDs (about Rs150 per page). The best option, however, may be to use the fax service at the government's local Central Telegraph Office. With private companies, you have to pay for faxes that don't transmit properly as long as a phone connection is made. At the government office, rates are cheaper to begin with (about Rs100) and the clerk will often try several times to get your fax through, without recharging you each time.

Telex messages can be sent from luxury hotels (again subject to a hefty service charge) or from main post offices which are relatively cheap. The advantage of the telex is that it gives you a record of any hotel bookings or airline confirmations made—a wise precaution in a country notorious for double-booking suites and seats.

Disabled Travellers

India is not a country which is easy to travel around if you have limited mobility, despite (and possibly because of) the fact that so many of her own population are disabled. Airlines and some major hotels are often helpful, but you can never rely on special facilities being available. For example, wheelchair ramps do not exist and access to bathrooms, restaurants and even hotel bedrooms is often impossible for those who cannot use stairs or pass through narrow doorways and passages. It may be possible to overcome these problems with the help of a companion.

The following organizations will be able to help you: **RADAR** (The Royal Association for Disability and Rehabilitation), 25 Mortimer Street, London W1N 8AB, ✆ (0171) 637 5400. In the USA: **American Foundation for the Blind**, 15 West 16th Street, New York, NY10011, ✆ (212) 620 2000; toll free ✆ 1-800 232 54631, and **SATD** (Society for the Advancement of Travel for the Disabled), Suite 610, 347 5th Avenue, New York, NY10016, ✆ (212) 447 7284.

Electricity

The electric current used in India is 220 volts AC, 50Hz. Sockets have two large round-pin holes. Current failures and power cuts are common all over India and you should expect the power to go out about once a day. It's a good idea to always carry candles or a torch with you in case of blackouts.

Embassies and Consulates

Most of the larger cities have consulates (listed in the telephone directory) but any major problems have to be resolved at the regional offices in Bombay:

UK: 2nd Floor, Hong Kong Bank Building, M.G. Road, Bombay ✆ 274874

USA: Lincoln House, 78 Bhulabhai Desai Road, Bombay ✆ 8223611

Australia: Maker Towers, B Block, 41 Cuffe Parade, Bombay ✆ 218071.

Festivals and Public Holidays

The Indian calendar is an ongoing procession of thousands of festivals each year. Nearly everywhere you go some sort of temple celebration, religious pageant or colourful arts festival will have just started or just ended. The major ones attract some of the best exponents of music, dance and theatre in the country. There are also vast crowds of hysterical devotees, so be careful.

There are no fixed dates for many of these festivals. Their timing is determined by the Indian lunar calendar and is calculable only during the previous year. Around October, your nearest Government of India tourist office should have the full list of festivals and dates for the forthcoming year. There are, however, a few national holidays when shops, banks and government offices are closed. Republic Day on **26 January**, Independence Day on **15 August** and Mahatma Gandhi's birthday on **2 October** are three days when everything is closed.

Some interesting and worthwhile festivals and fairs, together with their approximate dates, are listed below.

mid-Jan	**Pongal**. A major harvest festival involving lively processions, bullfights and much decorating of sacred cows. *Pongal* is a sweet rice preparation prepared from freshly harvested paddy.
late Jan	**The Feast of the Three Kings**, celebrated at various sites in Goa (the best is at Chandor) where a riotously drunken fair accompanies the procession.
26 Jan	**Republic Day**. A national holiday celebrated all over the country, marking India's adoption of their constitution.

mid-Feb	**Carnival**. Held in Goa, this non-religious celebration is similar to Mardi Gras, complete with feasting, drink and costumed revellers dancing in the street. General lunacy prevails.
mid-Feb–5th Sun in Lent	**Procession of the Saints**, Old Goa. The 26 icons inside the Church of St Andrew are paraded through a general fair with rides, booths and traditional dancing.
late March	**Holi**. This rowdy celebration of the advent of spring is quite an eyeful—everybody pelts everyone else with coloured water and powder, and hapless tourists are fair game.
mid-April	**Ramnavami**. The birthday of Lord Rama is celebrated by reciting the epic Ramayana in homes and temples throughout India.
late April	**The Feast of Our Lady of Miracles** (usually the Sunday two weeks after Easter). This is held at Mapusa and is accompanied by a large agricultural fair. It coincides with the local Hindu festival of the goddess Lairaiya.
June 13	**Feast of St Anthony**, celebrated in all churches through southern India. It welcomes the monsoon.
June 24	**Feast of St John the Baptist**. This is best celebrated at Calangute where the young men get drunk and run around jumping into wells!
June 29	**Festival of St Peter** at Fort Aguada. A procession of water-borne floats parades down the Mandovi River.
mid-July	**Teej**. Also to welcome the monsoons: women decorate swings with flowers.
15 Aug	**Independence Day**. The anniversary of India's independence from Britain is observed all over India.
mid-Aug	**The Harvest Festival** is celebrated at all churches but best of all in Panjim, where there is a re-enactment of the battle between Albequerque and the Adil Shahs, outside the Secretariat building.
Sept/Oct	**Dussehra**. A 10-day festival of national importance, celebrated everywhere.
2 Oct	**Gandhi Jayanti**. This national holiday marks the birth of Mahatma Gandhi.
Oct/Nov	**Diwali**. The liveliest and noisiest of all Indian festivals, a night-long revel of firecrackers and general pageantry

	celebrates Laxmi, the goddess of wealth and prosperity. Houses of the rich and poor glow beautifully with the light of special *diya* candles.
Nov/Dec	**International Seafood Festival**. This fair in Panjim, Goa, lets you sample the local seafood, as well as displaying Goan folk arts and crafts.
25 Dec	**Christmas Day**. Celebrated all over India with music and dance festivals, but best in Goa.

Food and Drink

Goan Cuisine

A delicious mixture of Asian and Western cooking, **Goan cuisine** is a popular escape from the usual south Indian diet of *thali*, *masala dosa* and curry. Long-term travellers flock here for the continental-style beach restaurants, with their pancakes, spaghetti, baked beans on toast and chips. New arrivals, unaware of the local pigs' diet of human faeces, tend to favour the traditional Goan pork sausages (*chourisso*) or classic pork dishes like *vindaloo* (marinated in toddy vinegar and very spicy) and *sorpatel* (pig's liver pickled in hot savoury sauce). *Xacuti* is a biting-hot coconut/*masala* preparation of chicken or mutton, and the rich, layered *bebinca* is a traditional, very filling Goan sweet made of coconut and jaggery. The other main fare is, of course, seafood. The Arabian Sea lapping Goa's coastline yields a variety of delicately flavoured fish and shellfish, including crab, oysters, king prawns, massive shark steaks and snapping-fresh lobsters.

Goa has the cheapest **beer** in India as well as the famous ***feni***, a smooth, potent brew (usually distilled just once) made from either the cashew apple or the coconut palm and sold for next to nothing. The local Goan **wines** are also popular and cheap, this being one of the few places in India where 'wine' shops actually sell wine, not just whisky.

South Indian Cuisine

South Indian food tends to be very spicy and also relies heavily on coconut. The base of almost every traditional meal is rice, rice and then more rice. When you order a 'meal' in a south Indian restaurant, you will invariably be given a huge portion of rice with various things to put on it: *sambar*, a thin, mild, vegetable and lentil soup spiced with tamarind; *rasam*, a hot and savoury thin soup; a vegetable mixture of some sort, for instance green beans with coconut; and curd. You will also be served *poori*, a small fried bread to help scoop up your rice. Most 'meals' include unlimited portions, and you may have to put your hand firmly over your plate to refuse second or third helpings. You can also get a variety of prepared rice dishes such as *pulao*, made with tamarind and ground nuts, or *pulav*, made with chopped vegetables.

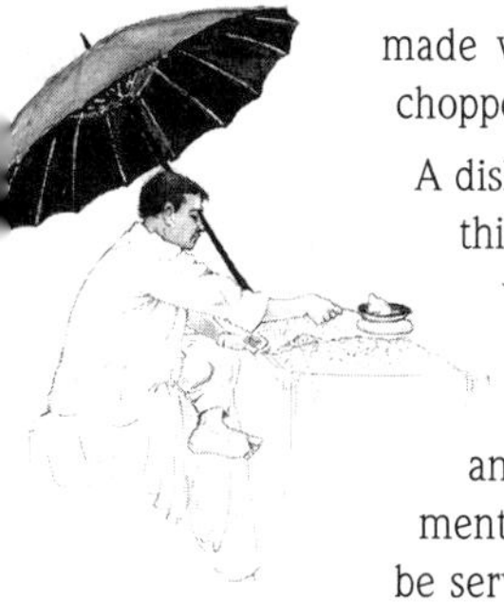

A dish that is particularly associated with the south is *dosa*, a thin, fried pancake made from rice and lentils. When filled with spicy potato and vegetable curry, it is called a *masala dosa*, when prepared with onions and hot chillies, it is called an *onion dosa*, prepared as a thicker and chewier pancake it is a *set dosa*, and made with fermented dough, it becomes a *rava dosa*. A *dosa* will normally be served with a delicious coconut-based chutney and sometimes a spicy vegetable mixture as well. *Dosa* is incredibly cheap, around Rs10, and very filling. Also famous in the south are *idli*, delicate and subtle-tasting mounds of sticky rice flour, served with *sambar*. *Chaat* is the name given to a variety of spicy and savoury snacks served in the south which can be combined to make a wonderful meal. Look for *bhel puri*, a spicy, sweet and sour puffed rice mixture, *masala puri*, a green spicy sauce with peas, yogurt and bits of fried pastry, *pani puri*, fried round pastry shells filled with onions, tomatoes, and coriander, or *sev dahi potato puri*, fried round pastry shells filled with potato and topped with a savoury sauce. Most *chaat* items only cost between Rs5 and Rs10, so just try anything on the menu that looks intriguing and see what appears!

Indian desserts or sweetmeats are very sweet—often seeming to be little more than coloured sugar cubes. *Gulub jamun*, a fried doughnut in syrup, is good but amazingly rich. Some people love traditional Indian desserts like *barfi*, a sweet coconut mixure, *jalebi*, small snail-shaped pancakes dripping with syrup, and milk/curd-based sweetmeats like *rasgulla* and *sandesh*, whereas others would rather eat an old shoe. The best Indian sweet, however, at least according to some addicts, is *chikki*, sold on every street corner. Similar to peanut brittle, but with a higher peanut-to-brittle ratio, this wonderful sweet can keep you going for days. The quality of *chikki* varies but good *chikki* should be crisp and not stick to your teeth.

Fresh fruit is one of the best things about India. Mangoes, pineapples, bananas (five or six different varieties), melons, coconuts and tangerines are widely sold in markets or by street vendors. And it's all ridiculously cheap. It's often a bad idea to buy fruit and vegetables (e.g. cucumbers) cut into segments and sold on the street because they attract too many flies. Always buy complete fruits and peel them yourself, or have the vendor cut open a new fruit for you. You'll soon get used to the luxury of never having to go more than a few paces to buy a piece of fruit. And the more fruit you eat the better, as your body seems to crave the vitamins after the strain of constantly moving about.

Drinks

The most popular beverage by far in India is *chai* or tea. Brewed up on every street corner, for Rs1 or Rs2 a shot, it usually appears as a glass of strong, filmy, dark brown liquid. *Chai* is commonly made with boiled buffalo milk and is loaded with sugar. You come to crave the stuff after a while even if you normally take your tea black at home, because it gives you an undeniable energy boost. You can order black tea at restaurants, however, if desired. Some travellers give up on tea completely and switch to coffee. This is often very good in the south and is available from Indian coffee-houses in most towns and cities.

One of the best drinks to have when you're hot and thirsty is a tender coconut. Sold everywhere at little stalls, these large green coconuts are filled with an unbelievable amount of cool, delicately flavoured coconut milk. They cost about Rs5 and the flesh on the inside of the shell can also be eaten (the vendor will usually split the coconut in half for you, and give you a sliver of the husk with which to scoop out the flesh). Indian doctors swear by tender coconuts as a general health aid, and they are supposed to be especially good for those with stomach problems. To replace all the fluids you will sweat out in the heat, remember to drink lots of bottled water. Numerous street kiosks sell litre bottles of mineral water for Rs10–15. Drinking bottled water will also help ensure that the water you drink is safe—just make sure the seal on the bottle is intact.

Alcoholic drinks are relatively cheap in Goa as long as you stick to Indian brands, which are generally of a lower quality but are passable.

Eating Out

At a high-class restaurant, particularly in the large international hotels, you can expect to pay anything beween Rs150–400 for a meal which outside would probably cost a quarter of that. Smart hotel restaurants also levy a 20% expenditure tax and the food is rarely worth it. If you look around, you can often find less expensive, better quality restaurants aimed at tourists and middle-class Indians which will certainly offer better fare than hotel food.

However, most restaurants charge about Rs60–80 per head, including a couple of drinks, and in the cheap *thali* houses in the towns you can generally eat *dosa* or rice *thali* for about Rs20 per head.

In traditional south Indian restaurants food is eaten with the hands only. This looks strange at first, especially since soupy rice forms the base of most meals, but Indians swear that food tastes better eaten this way and that spices can't be mixed properly into rice with a utensil. Try eating with your hands a few times. Where else will you get the opportunity to do so in public? All restaurants provide a wash basin to clean your hands both before and after eating. When eating out, you'll also notice that locals do all their eating with their right hand only (the left is used for something else). As a foreigner you can probably get away with using both hands without being laughed at, but learning how to tear a *poori* (a fried bread) with one hand gives a certain satisfaction.

Health and Insurance

You will need a course of vaccinations and a supply of malaria tablets for India. They are not essential requirements for entering the country but are very strongly recommended. A Yellow Fever Vaccination Certificate is required however if coming from a country recently infected with this disease. While sanitation and hygiene in India remain at their current levels, it's wise to take every possible precaution against ill-health.

Vaccinations

You'll need protection against typhoid, tetanus, polio and hepatitis. The cholera vaccine is now considered ineffective against the strains prevalent in India. Diseases like malaria and hepatitis, which are both very easily contracted, can not only make your life a misery while you are abroad but may also remain with you for the rest of your life.

In the UK you can either make an appointment to see your local GP or use a local vaccinating centre. Your GP is likely to be the cheapest option, but make sure you leave yourself enough time. London has several quick and efficient drop-in centres: **West London Vaccinating Centre** at 53 Great Cumberland Place, London W1H 7LH, ✆ (0171) 262 6456, open from 9am to 4.45pm; the **London Hospital for Tropical Diseases**, 4 St Pancras Way, London NW1 0PE, ✆ (0891) 600350; **Trailfinders**, 194 Kensington High Street, London W8 7RG, ✆ (0171) 938 3939; **British Airways Travel Clinic**, 156 Regent Street, London W1P 0LX ✆ (0171) 637 9899, open daily from 9am to 4.15pm, 10am to 12.30pm and 2pm to 4pm on Saturdays. Expect to pay up to £50 for a full course of injections at a commercial travel clinic.

General Precautions

Goa is not known for malaria but it is a potential danger and it is unwise not to take tablets; both the daily and weekly varieties. Start taking them 10 days before you leave for India. This gives you a chance to change them if the ones prescribed by the clinic or your GP don't agree with you; and it also allows your body to start building up some immunity before you arrive. Continue taking them for 6 weeks after returning home. To further reduce risks equip yourself with a mosquito net (useful even inside hotels), some coils to burn in hotel rooms and a good repellent such as **Jungle Formula**, to give you double protection. At night, wear trousers and a long-sleeved shirt.

Once you've seen the doctor, see your **dentist**. While dental treatment in the major cities is of a high standard and not expensive, facilities outside the major cities are often more basic.

Contact-lens wearers should consider switching to specs for India because of dust, heat, intense glare, etc. **Spectacle wearers** should note down their prescription. Opticians in India are cheap and the cost of prescription lenses and frames is often a fraction of the UK equivalent.

AIDS

AIDS in India is much more prevalent than is officially accepted. The problem is not confined to the 'red-light' areas of the major towns but is possibly spread throughout the country. Anyone seeking a working or student visa for more than one year must take an AIDS test and submit a copy of the certificate verifying a negative result along with the visa application.

Travel and Medical Insurance

You don't have to believe everything you hear about theft and illness in India, but you can't afford to ignore it either. Good travel insurance is essential for your peace of mind and has saved many travellers a lot of heartache. Take great care when choosing your policy and always read the small print. A good travel insurance should give full cover for your possessions and health. In case of illness, it should provide for all medical costs, hospital benefits, permanent disabilities and the flight home. In case of theft or loss it should recompense you for lost luggage, money and valuables and also for travel delay and personal liability. Most important (and this could be a life-saver) it should provide you with a 24-hour contact number in the event of medical emergencies.

If your own bank or insurance company hasn't an adequate travel insurance scheme (they usually have), then try the comprehensive, but expensive schemes offered by **Trailfinders**, ✆ (0171) 938 3939, **Jardine's**, ✆ (0161) 228 3742, or the Centurion Assistance policy (linked to Europ Assistance) offered by **American Express**, ✆ (01444) 239900. Travel companies often include insurance in the cost of a luxury tour but this is not always adequate. Whichever insurance you buy, take a copy of the policy with you to India. Most important, keep a separate note of the 24-hour emergency number and keep it on you at all times.

Should anything be stolen a copy of the police report or FIR (First Information Report) should be asked for and retained. A copy of the police report may be required by your insurance company when making a claim.

Money

Visitors are normally asked to declare the amount of foreign currency in their possession upon arrival in India. Those having more than US$10,000 in the form of travellers' cheques or bank notes are required to obtain a **Currency Declaration Form** before leaving Customs. This will ensure that you can reconvert any excess rupees upon departure. You will also need encashment certificates for the reconversion (*see* below).

Remember that you *cannot take rupees into or out of India*; you have to exchange them within the country. It is wise to bring most of your money in travellers' cheques as they can be refunded if lost or stolen, but a small amount of cash (about US$100) is useful in emergencies. You should always change your money into rupees at authorized money changers or banks. It is illegal to exchange money through unauthorized channels and sometimes people offering to change money on the street are actually police informers. Moreover, the street rate of exchange is often lower than the official bank rate.

Save the **encashment certificates** which official money changers issue for all transactions. These are needed to reconvert rupees into your original currency before leaving the country. Rupees cannot be reconverted once outside of India.

It is recommended you buy **American Express** or **Thomas Cook travellers' cheques** because they have many offices around India and have good reputations for swift, efficient refunding in the event of loss. Other companies do not always refund losses immediately. American Express has offices/agents in Bombay: 276 Dr Dadabhai Naoroji Road, Majithia Chambers, © 2048291/8295. Thomas Cook has offices in Bombay, Dr Dadabhai Naoroji Road, © 2048556/8; Cochin, Palal Towers, 1st floor, Right Wing, © 369829; and Panjim, 8 Alcon Chambers, Dayanand Bandodkar Marg, © 221312. Make sure that the travellers' cheque company you do choose gives you (in writing) the addresses of their refunding agents in India. Sign your travellers' cheques immediately on receipt and make a separate note of the cheque numbers. Store these numbers separately from the cheques and mark down which cheques you cash as you go along. In case your cheques are stolen, you will then be able to get them replaced with minimum hassle.

Budgeting Your Trip

If you're on a shoestring, Rs350–500 per day will cover basic accommodation, food, bus or 2nd class rail travel and even leave enough for a beer at the end of the day. If you want to shop, eat well and stay in air-conditioned accommodation as well as travel by luxury coach or 2nd class air-conditioned train, allow for Rs1000 per day. If you want to use 5-star hotels, hotel restaurants and private cars, allow for a *minimum* of Rs3000–5000 per day.

Price ranges are often misleading: you don't need to spend a lot of money to ensure cleanliness and comfort. There is often little difference (except in cost!) between 5-star hotels and more moderate accommodaton. Similarly, the most expensive restaurants are often the most bland. Explore the hotels and restaurants in the 'moderate' and 'inexpensive' categories of this guide and you will have a more interesting trip, stay healthy and save money.

Credit Cards

In India the American Express card justifies its additional expense by enabling you toget into hotels if you've just lost all your money, but a Visa card is probably more useful—airlines and big hotels accept it, as do most travel agents. Some banks will give you a **cash advance** on Visa cards—among them the State Bank of Andhra and Grindlays Bank. Making purchases on your credit card is not a bad idea, as most credit card companies offer a competitive exchange rate and do not charge you any commission on the transaction.

Running Out of Money

This is another good reason to bring credit cards, as getting money wired over through the banks is slow and painful. It's not completely unknown for banks to keep the money in their system for up to three weeks before admitting that it has arrived. A good travel agent may advance you money if you put up your passport as security—but only if they know you. Always keep US$100 cash stashed away somewhere safe in the event of losing the bulk of your money. If you find yourself really desititute, head for the nearest Sikh temple. These have a law of hospitality similar to some Christian monasteries, and you will be fed and sheltered until rescue arrives.

Opening Hours

For **business opening hours** there are no rules: shopkeepers stay open as long as they can to make the most of the trade, shutting only on religious holidays. Even on public holidays you will find some shops open. The same cannot be said of **government offices**, which open from 9 to 5 only and shut at weekends. The only exceptions are the **central telegraph offices** in the larger towns, which stay open until midnight, allowing you to take advantage of cheap rates for long-distance telephone calls. However, all government offices shut for religious and public holidays. Goa's **bars** stay open until the small hours.

Packing

Goa's warm climate requires a minimum of clothing. The wisest travellers take only one change of clothes and buy whatever else they need out there: India's **hand-woven cotton textiles** are dirt cheap, beautifully made and let the skin breathe much better than their European counterparts. The same applies to Indian **leather sandals**. To kit yourself out on arrival head straight for Anjuna or Mapusa Market.

Backpackers should definitely have a **waterbottle**, **water-purification tablets**, a good **penknife** and a light **mosquito net**. The latter gives perfect protection whether in hotel rooms or jungles from all crawly bitey things. You should also take good **insect repellent**, though if you forget you can buy a decent brand in India called Odomos. If you are going into any wild area take some good lightweight **hiking boots** and a small pair of **binoculars** for bird and game spotting—binoculars are also useful in large temples with intricate carvings on the high *gopurams* (towers). You should also buy all your **camera film** before your go as Indian brands sometimes give a greenish tinge to their prints and occasionally don't come out at all.

Buy all your **medical supplies** before you go including antiseptic spray to both dry and disinfect wounds at the same time, gauze and medical tape for dressings, your own hyperdermic needles, several tubes of antihistamine cream to stop you gouging itchy bites into open sores, a healthy supply of aspirin, lip balm and aloe vera gel to stop you peeling after getting sunburnt, as well as diarrhoea tablets and rehydration packs. High-potency **sunblock** is a necessity. Make sure you buy more than you will need before you go as it can be hard to find in India. Those who value their hair should also take a good **conditioner** with them as your hair tends to dry out in the heat and break off like straw after washing.

Security

Theft is a fairly common problem on the beaches but you can minimize the risk by observing a few simple precautions. If you are backpacking, invest in some small padlocks for your pocket zippers and never, but never, lose sight of your pack.

When booking into cheap lodges check that your door has a padlock and make sure your windows are shut when you go out, even if they have bars—where people may not be able to get in, monkeys often can!

Personal security is not really a problem in peaceable south India, except in some areas of the large towns after dark or when sleeping on the beaches in Goa or Karnataka—if you do either of these things, stay in a group and you'll be fine. In slums and villages dogs and monkeys are more likely to attack you than people. Carry a big stick: this will drive off most mammalian assailants if you hold your ground.

Shopping

India is one of the great markets of the world. You can find a remarkable range of fabulous produce, including silk, cotton, leather, jewellery, carving and handicrafts at real bargain prices, sometimes four or five times cheaper than abroad. The quality of craftsmanship is often excellent, and even if what you want is not in stock it can invariably be made up for you—either on the spot or sent on later.

Always try to start your shopping tour with a visit to a government or state emporium, such as the ones in Panjim and Margao. These stock the full range of local produce and handicrafts, sometimes with a selection of goods from neighbouring states. Because all prices are fixed, you are able to establish exactly what is available and how much it should cost. This knowledge can be invaluable when it comes to buying things in less scrupulous high street shops, markets or bazaars such as Anjuna's Wednesday flea market and the Friday market at Mapusa..

On the streets you'll have to bargain hard. The big thing to bear in mind is that there is always an Indian price and a tourist price. Offer half the asking price and work from there. If you are buying something bulky or valuable, ask for a certificate of origin and a receipt (essential when the article hits customs as it becomes very expensive if you can't produce it) and arrange for the item(s) bought to be shipped home for you. In case a completely different article turns up at your front door it can be a good idea to photograph or mark the item at the time of actually purchasing it.

Sports and Activities

Outdoor Activities

Goa's mountain forests offer some good **wildlife viewing**, (*see* p.58 for a full list of wildlife species), whether by vehicle or foot. The mountains also offer **trekking**, in jungles that have seen very few Western travellers; *see* p.117 for full details.

Good **swimming** can be found at any of the beaches listed in the guide, with the exception of the beach immediately next to Vasco da Gama. The big resort hotels offer **windsurfing** and other water sports. On Arambol and Anjuna beaches, you can sign up for a **parascending** course through the Shore Bar on Anjuna Beach. For full details *see* p.80.

For the specialist, the Indian **martial art** of Kalaripayat can be studied at the C.V.N. School in Trivandrum near Kovalam beach in Kerala, and there are lots of places nearby which teach **ayurvedic medicine and massage**.

Time

There are no time differences within India. Time differences between India and some major international cities are: Auckland +06:30; Berlin –04:30; London –05:30; Los Angeles –13:30; New York –10:30; Paris –04:30; Sydney +02:30; Toronto –09:00.

Tourist Information

There are national and state tourist offices in most of the larger Goan towns which vary considerably in their degree of efficiency. The best is probably the office in Margao but there are others in Panjim, Mapusa and Vasco da Gama:

Panjim Tourist Office, Tourist Hostel (by the jetty), © (0832) 223396/224063

Margao Tourist Office, Tourist Hostel, Miranda Road, © (0834) 222513

Mapusa Tourist Office, Tourist Shopping Complex, © (0832) 262390

Vasco da Gama Tourist Office, Tourist Hostel, off Swantantra Path, © (0834) 512673.

Where to Stay

This book lists price categories for accommodation, per room, per night, as follows:

luxury:	over Rs1500 in small towns, beaches and the country side; over Rs3000 in the major resorts
expensive:	Rs750–1500
moderate:	Rs350–750
inexpensive:	Rs100–350
cheap:	under Rs100

Note: these prices were valid at the time of publication. Expect a 10–20 per cent rise in tariffs for each subsequent year.

Hotels

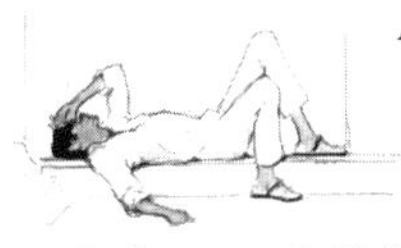

As a general rule the further south you go in India, the cheaper accommodation becomes. In Goa and Kovalam, prices rise by 25 per cent in the holiday, or 'high' season, from November to February, but outside these months you will be able to bargain for up to half the advertised rates.

Officially, foreign guests in all hotels in India are charged in dollars but in practice most hotels below the luxury category only have a rupee tariff. Even in 5-star hotels you can often pay in rupees against an encashment certificate—the hotel staff may be unwilling to allow this but if faced with no choice they are not going to refuse your money in whatever form it comes.

The 'luxury' resorts, such as the Leela Beach Resort at Cavelossim or Fort Aguada north of Panjim charge prices on a par with the West. One night in a top resort can cost as much as Rs5000 (about £100 or US$160)—for this you can expect a smart air-conditioned double suite (probably with private balcony and view), access to a good swimming pool and a number of useful facilities such as watersports, a shopping arcade, travel agency, bank, two or three restaurants, in-house entertainments, car park, beauty parlour and health club. Car hire and sightseeing tours are also often arranged. Away from the main resort beaches the standard of luxury hotels varies markedly but the prices are far lower—averaging about Rs1500 per room per night in 1995/6.

Hotels in the 'expensive' category vary tremendously—the price is seldom an indication of quality. Often a town's best hotel will fall into a lower price bracket than this, and you should choose your accommodation according to the comments in each 'Where to Stay' section of the guide (or from other travellers) rather than expecting automatic value for money.

A double room in a decent 'moderate' category hotel will often buy the same facilities as an expensive one—air-conditioning, attached restaurant, some sort of room service and (occasionally) a room telephone. Equally good but usually lacking in air-conditioning are the 'inexpensive' hotels—often the best value but occasionally appalling. To avoid staying somewhere awful, follow the recommendations in the guide closely and only stay somewhere that is not recommended as a last resort.

Before you take a room in a 'cheap' hotel or rent a one-room cottage from a family, give it a thorough once-over for cleanliness and for facilities. In economy places you can perhaps overlook the chipped basins, the peeling plaster and old coffee stains on walls. However, do not overlook the following check list: dirty bed linen; bedbugs under mattresses; cockroaches in bathrooms and waste bins. Expect to use an outside toilet, to wash by bucket from a well and to use candles at night.

Women Travellers

India is one of the world's safest countries to travel in and few women experience any serious danger here, unless out on their own after dark when Indian men become drunker and bolder. However, 'Eve-teasing', as the Indians call sexual harassment of women, can be a common sport among groups of Indian men. This is almost always confined to stares and rude remarks but women may find themselves groped in crowds. If this happens don't be afraid to make a scene or even strike your molester—public opinion will certainly be on your side.

Ways to avoid unwanted attention are: don't smoke in public—this is a sign of a 'loose woman'; don't wear short shorts or leave the whole arm uncovered when out in public; don't respond to persistent questioning—learn to be rude, everyone else in India is. If you go topless on the beaches in Goa or Kerala you just have to expect crowds of men to gather—bare breasts are almost never seen in India and the sight of a pair will stop a whole street.

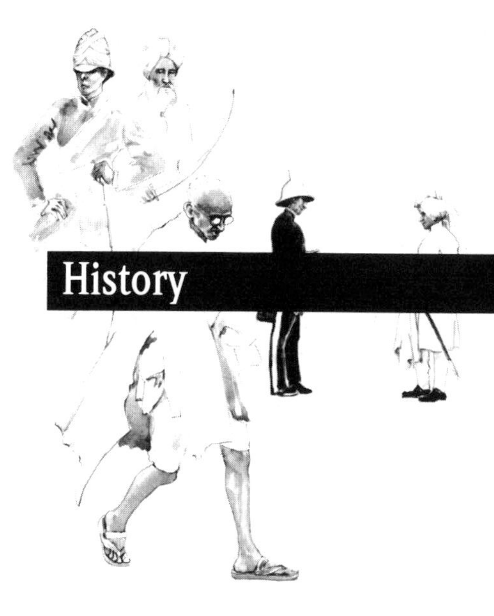

History

A lucky venture, a lucky venture! Plenty of rubies, plenty of emeralds! You owe great thanks to God for having brought you to a country holding such riches!

An Indian welcome to the first Portuguese, from *The Route to India 1497–8, Portuguese Voyages.*

Ancient Goa

Hindus believe that Goa was reclaimed from the sea by the sixth avatar (incarnation) of Vishnu. Most historians agree that the ancestors of the modern Indian Goans were descendants of the first generation of Aryan invaders, a Middle Eastern people who invaded northern India in about 1500 BC, their cavalry and chariots overrunning the great Indus Valley civilization that had flourished in northern and western India over the previous 3 millennia. The Aryans are thought to have reached Goa in about AD 600, where they subjugated and then intermarried with the aboriginal tribal people, building small towns and forts and carving out petty chiefdoms along the lush, sub-tropical coast.

Historical records first mention Goa in the 3rd century BC when it was the province of Aparanta, part of the short-lived Mauryan Empire of northern India. After the fall of the Mauryans the Andhran dynasty took over the region but showed little interest in Goa, regarding it as a backwater compared with the more cosmopolitan eastern coast of India, which had trade links with the Far East. This allowed a local Goan dynasty, the Kadambas, to emerge, its rulers descended from the local governors of the Andhran Empire.

The Kadamba monarchs first governed as client kings under the powerful Pallava dynasty of Tamil Nadu, great temple builders and traders who took Goa from the Andhras in about AD 250 and dominated all of southern India until AD 500. The Kadambas acquired a nominal kind of independence during the last 100 years of Pallava rule. But their freedom was short-lived; in the 6th century, the Pallavas were overrun by their Deccan rivals, the Chalukyans and, again, the Kadambas shrewdly allied themselves with the dominant force.

The Konkan, as Goa was now known, managed to escape the great wars that raged across southern India between the 6th and 10th centuries as various minor dynasties and invaders challenged Chalukyan rule. The Kadambas profited from this peaceful period on the political sidelines. Records state that during the late 10th century they founded a great capital city called Gopakkatattana, its site thought to be under or near modern Old Goa. The Kadambas were growing rich on a new trade route—since the rise of Islam in the 7th century the focus of Indian maritime commerce had shifted from the Far East to Arabia and Goa was in a prime position to exploit this. Moreover, Arabia, and therefore Goa, could supply the warlike Chalukyan overlords with the commodity they most needed to maintain their military supremacy—Arabian horses. From the 10th century onwards Goa, or the Konkan, began to emerge as an independent state.

Horse Traders to the Deccan Princes

Goa continued to flourish throughout the 11th century. With the arrival of the Muslims in India, the Kadambas were again lucky in remaining on the peaceful sidelines of a turbulent time. While northern India was overrun by savage Islamic invaders, Goa and the south enjoyed a completely peaceful relationship with the Muslims of Arabia. Many Arab traders settled in Goa and the other southern coastal regions, their religion tolerated by the local Hindus.

Goa was also sufficiently distant from the Deccan Plateau to make direct rule impossible to enforce, particularly as their Chalukyan overlords were fully occupied in fighting endless campaigns against rival dynasties. The Kadamba governors began to supply horses not only to their feudal lords but to their enemies as well, safe in the knowledge that the Chalukyans were too dependent on a steady supply of horses to risk disrupting the trade and too wary of their Deccan enemies to lay siege to the ports and risk an attack in the rear. By the late 1100s Goa had become a fully separate kingdom.

In 1293 the Italian traveller and adventurer Marco Polo visited the horse-trading cities of the Malabar Coast and remarked of the main Goan port (probably near modern Vasco da Gama): 'Accordingly, all the ships coming from the west—as from Ormus, Christi, Aden and various parts of Arabia—laden with merchandise and horses, make this port. The prince maintains in the most splendid manner no fewer than 300 women.' Lucky old prince. But the booming trade and consequent affluence attracted pirates too. Marco Polo also described these: 'Numerous pirates scour those seas [of Malabar] with more than 100 vessels. They take with them their wives and children, who continue to accompany them during the whole summer's cruise.' This gentle piracy even extended to sparing the lives of the merchants. Instead of being killed, Polo wrote that they were sent back to the coast 'to provide themselves with another cargo which, in case of their passing that way again, may be the means of enriching their captors a second time'.

So the Goa of the 13th century seems to have been an exceptionally peaceful place, but this was not to last. Soon after Marco Polo passed through, south India suffered its first Mughal invasions, which came in waves between 1296 and 1325. These were limited to raiding campaigns and for the moment they passed Goa by. But the Mughal generals came to know of the rich coastal cities and their valuable horse trade. In 1328 the Delhi sultan, Muhammed Shah, sent a vast army south and sacked Goa along with just about every other city of southwest India. The main Mughal army did not stay in Goa, but the Deccan was divided up between various sultanates, all anxious to profit from the trade. It was the end for the Kadambas and for Hindu rule.

Invasions and Atrocities

The first Deccan sultans to try their luck with a full conquest of Goa were the Bahmani sultans of Bidar on the northeast Deccan, who sent an army in the early 1350s. Like the Mughals of northern India, the Bahmanis were fervently anti-Hindu and during their occupation of Goa they put to death thousands of Kadamba subjects, destroyed temples and replaced them with mosques.

These religious atrocities enraged the Deccan's last great Hindu dynasty, the Vijayanagars of central and southern Karnataka, who had risen to power during the early 14th century and established a large capital at Hampi, about 200 miles east of Goa's mountain border. The Vijayanagars had already fought various campaigns against the Bahmani sultans and lost no time in launching an expedition to drive them from Goa. It was successful; by about 1380 most of the coast was garrisoned by Vijayanagar troops and the horse trade was back in the hands of the Hindus. The Muslim traders, who had kept out of the Bahmani persecutions, were allowed to stay, but the Bahmani mosques were razed and the old temples reconsecrated.

Goa remained a Vijayanagar province until 1469 when the Bahmanis launched a massive reconquest. The Bahmani Empire had swallowed several neighbouring sultanates during the 1450s and 60s and by the time it moved against Goa it could field far more soldiers than the Vijayanagars, despite the Hindu kings' superiority in cavalry. Using war elephants, field guns and siege engines that could hurl rocks of over 300lbs into the enemy ranks, the Bahmanis, under their invincible general Mahmud Gawan, sacked the Vijayanagars' Goan capital of Gova so severely that no trace of it survives today. Once again thousands of Hindus were put to the sword and a new Muslim Goan capital was laid out at Ela on the Mandovi River, near modern Goa Velha.

The new Bahmani rule was short-lived, but not the Muslim occupation. By 1490 internal divisions in the royal house at Bidar allowed a breakaway dynasty, called the Adil Shahs, to emerge from the family who governed the province of Bijapur in northern-central Karnataka. With the revolt of Bijapur the governors of the eastern province of Golconda, near modern Hyderabad, also rebelled and the Bahmani dynasty fell. The Adil Shahs took control of Goa, built themselves a palace on the site of the present Secretariat in Panjim and settled down to enjoy its wealth.

Enter the Portuguese

But like the Bahmanis the Adil Shahs were not destined to keep Goa for long. A new and aggressively anti-Muslim power was shortly to wrest Goa from their control. Throughout the 15th century the Portuguese, following their conquest of the Moorish city of Ceuta near modern Tangiers in 1415, had been sailing progressively south along the coast of Africa, establishing trading posts on the Gold Coast and searching for a way to the East. In the late 1480s the Portuguese mariner Bartholomeu Diaz rounded the Cape of Good Hope and crossed from the Atlantic into the Indian Ocean. A second voyage put out from Lisbon in 1497 under Vasco da Gama. Sailing round the Cape and up the East African coast, da Gama eventually found Christian Indian mariners at Malindi in Kenya who agreed to pilot him across to the Malabar Coast.

The first Portuguese landfall was at Calicut in northern Kerala, another horse-trading centre, though of less importance than Goa. Da Gama's men were met by Moorish merchants at Calicut who immediately demanded of them in Andalucian Spanish: 'May the Devil take ye, ye infidels. What brought you hither?' Unfazed, the Portuguese quickly made an alliance with the ruler of Calicut, agreeing to aid him against the other cities of the Keralan coast, with whom there was continual, low-level warring for control of the southern routes across the Arabian Sea. But the Portuguese soon fell foul of Calicut (in 1500) when they made similar military alliances with the rulers of Cochin and Cannanore, rivals of Calicut. A fort was built in Cochin in 1502 and a Portuguese viceroy sent out to govern it. Envoys were sent inland to the Vijayanagar court and a tentative alliance was established between the Europeans and the Deccan Hindus, who hoped that the Portuguese might help them regain a foothold on the coast.

The Malabar coast's Muslim traders, fearing this expansion of Portuguese interests, launched a Goan fleet against Cochin in 1509. It was defeated, and the Portuguese sent galleons in pursuit of the second Muslim fleet as it headed home to Goa, at the same time alerting the Vijayanagars in Hampi that Goa was vulnerable to attack. The Portuguese ships—under Albuquerque, Portuguese India's second and most pugnacious viceroy—blockaded the Adil Shahs' palace and took Ela. The force was too small to withstand the Adil Shahs' first counter-attack and the Portuguese were forced to leave the city a few weeks later, but they now determined to annex the territory. In 1512 a much larger fleet successfuly captured and held Ela. Goa was now a Portuguese colony, complete wth resident viceroy and army and Portuguese warships controlled the whole northern Malabar Coast.

With the Portuguese sword came the cross. In Kerala the first mariners had encountered Syrian Orthodox Christians (which miffed them as they had hoped for a fresh country to convert), the people of Goa, however, were either Hindu or Muslim and the priests who had come out with the soldiers and traders revelled in what seemed an open field for evangelism.

At first the Goan clergy took a philanthropic approach. Soldiers were encouraged to marry the local beauties (as long as the women converted) with no loss of status for the children who resulted from their unions. Low-caste Hindus flocked to convert, hoping to transcend the limitations of their birth (though in fact the caste system managed to adapt to Christianity). But as the colony prospered the Church gradually became more established and conservative. The first Jesuits arrived in the early 1540s, including the zealous evangelist St Francis Xavier (now buried in the Basilica of Bom Jesus) and began to rail against any tolerance of idolatry.

The colonists also became more aggressive, annexing Bardez and Salcete *talukas* in the later 1540s and destroying mosques and temples as they went —just as the first Muslim invaders had done back in the 14th century. Churches were built on the pagan sites and the first magnificent cathedrals and basilicas of Old Goa were begun. Goa got its own archbishop in 1558 and two years later the Inquisition arrived. Goa's Muslim traders and Hindu townsfolk suddenly found themselves stripped of all rights and privilege. With the first *autos-da-fe* they realized with horror that they now had to choose between forced conversion, exile with the loss of all their property or death.

But Portuguese rule did not go unchallenged. So great was the ill-feeling against the Europeans that the Hindu and Muslim princes of the Deccan actually allied—an unprecedented burying of the hatchet brought about by the rapidly growing power of the new Portuguese colony and its maddening control of the horse trade upon which both the Vijayanagars and Adil Shahs relied, as had all Deccan princes before them.

For a while it seemed as though the combined army might take Goa, but ancient enmity between the Hindus and Muslims provided a respite for the Portuguese as, instead of co-operating with the Vijayanagars for the final push, Bijapur decided to do away with them so that Bijapur could annex the coast for itself. In 1565 the Adil Shahs and the other main Deccan sultanates including Golconda attacked and defeated a huge Vijayanagar army at their capital of Hampi, sacking the place so ferociously that the site has remained a ruin to this day. It seemed nothing could stop the massed Muslim armies from descending on the Portuguese and sweeping them into the sea. Yet the internecine conflicts of the Deccan rulers interceded once again. Bijapur, Golconda and the other sultanates fell out over the spoils from Hampi and their subsequent petty wars allowed Goa to profit from the removal of its two greatest rivals. Apart from the irritating arrival (in 1580) of Dutch colonists in Kerala, Goa's control of the Arabian sea routes was now uncontested.

Goa Dorada

The hundred years that followed the fall of the Vijayanagars marked Goa's 'Golden Age'. Despite a bit of competition from the Dutch the Goan trade with Arabia was supplemented by new routes to the Far East—to Malaysia, the Philippines and even Japan and China. Goa was now the easternmost capital of Christendom and one of its richest, despatching scores of revenue-bearing ships to Lisbon every year. In return, Lisbon sent out thousands of colonists to replace the many victims of malaria and the periodic cholera epidemics.

It was a time of splendid cultural achievement. From the late 16th to the late 17th centuries the colony raised vast ecclesiastical buildings decorated with the latest Baroque interiors. Seminaries such as those at Rachol and Pilar (*see* pp.107 and 93) flourished as centres of learning and attracted scholars from Europe. The Jesuits of Rachol printed the first bibles in the Konkani language and began distributing them through Goa and the Deccan. The Portuguese poet Luis Vaz de Camões was so moved by the splendour of what he saw in Goa that he wrote his nation's great epic, the *Lusiad* (a praise-poem of the Portuguese people in similar style to Classical Rome's *Aeneid*), which has survived to the present day as one of the literary classics of the Renaissance.

Camões was not the only writer to compare 'Golden Goa' with Rome and even the colonists themselves conspired to keep up the idea: contemporary chroniclers report that the viceroys of the late 16th and early 17th centuries, still involved in petty wars with Indian rulers up and down the Malabar Coast would be given Roman triumphs on returning from their campaigns, riding in a chariot through the main streets of the city over which carpets had been thrown, their heads crowned with a wreath of laurels in imitation of the Roman proconsuls of the Late Republic. But not all the comparisons with Rome were so glorious: the colony had almost unlimited slave labour and as the 17th century progressed the Portuguese began to slip into a life of decadent ease rivalling that of Rome during its decline.

And Goa's fortunes were indeed soon to decline. While the wealth of the city soared and the Church celebrated its power with the state-sponsored horrors of the Inquisition, Portuguese galleons fought repeated bloody sea-battles with the Dutch. From 1605 Holland began to acquire more and more territory along the southern Malabar Coast and around the Portuguese possessions in the Far East. The Dutch were only held at bay by a Portuguese-English alliance of 1635, which resulted in a further treaty with Holland in 1668. However, this did not prevent Dutch shipping from poaching as much Portuguese trade as possible.

The Imperial Twilight

It was also time for a reckoning on land. In the early 1670s a French missionary called the Abbé Carré visited Goa and found it in a mess. The Inquisition had become so powerful that it was even persecuting its own clergy. The bishop of Bicholim in northern Goa was forced to surround himself with Muslim soldiers for protection against his vicious archbishop, who considered him a heretic. The Abbé arrived in Old Goa itself on Christmas day and, hoping to hear Mass, went straight to the Se Cathedral, only to find it shut. He then went around all the other churches, only to find the same thing and finally resorted to banging on the doors of the monasteries. However, all the orders turned him away with insults. In his report of the governing Portuguese of the time, Carré uses words such as 'effeminate, cowardly and immoral'. Obviously the once proud imperial city was rotting from the inside.

It seemed that the Portuguese had grown foolishly confident; they had survived the Dutch threat, and the sultans of Bijapur were no longer powerful enough to offer any kind of threat, indeed the Abbé Carré on a trip into the Deccan found the Bijapuri kingdom in a worse state than Goa, the Shah having just died and his country collapsing into civil war). However, a new and much more dangerous threat was descending on Goa.

Through the late 1660s and early 1670s a new Hindu force, the Marathas, had risen in the Deccan. Under their charismatic leader Shivaji, these fierce cavalry fighters began to expand their territories from their heartland near Pune in Maharashtra, to the north of Goa. They advanced southward to annex parts of the old southern Deccan sultanates, such as Bijapur, and north to conquer the southernmost regions of the Mughal sultanates of Delhi. By the late 1670s Maratha horsemen had already spilled into Goa, but as yet they had been content with tribute and refrained from ravaging the countryside or attacking the Portuguese. In fact the Goan viceroys, despite their decadence, managed to remain on cordial diplomatic terms with both the Marathas and the Mughals until 1679. The threat of a much larger Mughal/Maratha war loomed and the Goans were suspected of partiality by both sides. The Marathas attacked in 1680.

This episode was marked by Goa's only recorded miracle. The colonial army went to meet the Hindu cavalry but was routed. The city of Goa was besieged and all seemed lost. With the Marathas beating at the gates, the viceroy—unable to think of anything else—asked for divine help. After praying at the tomb of St Francis Xavier in the Basilica of Bom Jesus, the viceroy placed his staff of office inside the glass casket next to the dead saint along with a letter asking him to intercede with God and save the colony from destruction. Next day news came to the besieging Marathas that an army from Delhi was coming to attack them in the rear. The hostile forces withdrew and the city was saved.

However, Goa's trade was now in serious decline. From the early 1700s the city fell into semi-dereliction with only the ecclesiastical and government buildings properly maintained. There was still commercial activity but on a much-reduced scale, and renewed cholera epidemics were stripping the colony of settlers.

The Emergence of Modern Goa

The Portuguese (or rather their Rajput mercenaries) managed to defend their city and coastal forts well enough for the Marathas (who had won their war with Delhi) to finally agree to peace talks in 1739. The result of the treaty was that Goa, although impoverished, finally managed to extend its official boundaries right up to the Western Ghats, establishing the modern state of Goa. This achieved, the viceregal administration adopted an enlightened style of government. The Inquisition was abolished in 1760, and from this point on the colony began to let go of its old mercantile ambition and became more akin to today's rural backwater with the Jesuits developing the cultivation of coconut and cashew along the coast.

As Britain expanded its Indian territories in the early 1800s, Goa, protected by a Portuguese-British alliance, could happily forget any threat of invasion, whether Indian or European. The Goans had to put up with the periodic garrisoning of British troops in some of their coastal forts but the days of war were past. Britain honoured Portugal's claim under the later British Raj and Portuguese power remained essentially intact right up to December 1961, when its Indian lands finally returned to Indian control.

The early 19th century saw the gradual but complete abandonment of Old Goa, and a new period of building began in healthier Panjim. In 1835 all religious orders, except for the Carmelite nuns, were expelled from Goa and the church receded considerably in importance. Various notable Indian Goans began to think seriously about demanding independence for the territory. The colonial government's military weakness was highlighted by several successful uprisings of the Rajput mercenaries when attempts were made to force higher taxes on them or to strip them of their special privileges. In the 1850s and 60s several liberal newspapers were established and the Indo-Portuguese journalist Luis de Menenzes Braganza (part of a wealthy ex-Hindu family whose superb villa in Chandor can now be visited) became the leading light of a nationalist movement that began to put considerable pressure on Lisbon in the early 1900s.

In 1928 a grandson of Luis de Menenzes Braganza formed the Goan National Congress, which allied with the Indian National Congress in the 1930s, and Independence was now an inevitability. Lisbon was keen to be rid of the now unwieldy colony, and only bureaucratic muddlings kept Portugal from letting go of Goa soon after India's seccession from Britain in 1947. The colonial administration was slowly dismantled throughout the 1950s and in 1961 Nehru, India's first prime minister, finally lost patience and sent in troops. The old threat of invasion from Delhi had finally materialized. Goa's small Portuguese garrison surrendered (rather relievedly, one suspects) and Goa was finally a part of India again.

The transfer of Goa from European back to Indian hands was not without an element of farce. A common story among children of the old settlers (now living back in Portugal) is that the Goan garrison only surrendered because it had no guns, barring some ancient pre-war firearms that had rusted into oblivion. According to the story, the garrison commander had arranged with Lisbon that guns were to be sent out some weeks before the arrival of Indian troops on Goan soil, but the request had been written in code with *chourissos* (sausages) replacing the word 'guns'. Unfortunately the cipher to the code was misplaced and the garrison was duly supplied with a shipload of *chourissos* from Lisbon with which to welcome the Indian force. History relates that the reconquest went off without a shot fired, but there is no record of whether or not the Portuguese and Indian soldiers sat down to a meal of *chourissos* together.

During the last 30 years Goa's Indo-Portuguese character has remained essentially unchanged. The Portuguese themselves have gone but they have left behind them a new ruling class of Indo-Portuguese landowners. Being part of India has brought Goa considerable economic benefits. The Portuguese did little for the territory—until 1961 there were no bridges, no roads (just bullock tracks once out of Panjim) and no electricity. The Indians built bridges over Goa's principal rivers, the Mandovi and the Zuari, and Panjim was at last linked with north and south Goa. They also developed Pilar Harbour—a vast natural harbour backing onto a coastal mountain rich in iron ore—and Goa became wealthy practically overnight.

Finally, having constructed paved roads, modern buildings, hotels and proper communications, the Indian Government prepared Goa for tourism. The potential was always there—the charming little villages with their sunny piazzas, the unbroken miles of sandy beaches, the pretty whitewashed churches and chapels and the exotic combination of the Latin and Indian. But it was only in the 1960s with the arrival of the hippies that Goa's vast tourist market was at last recognized.

The Goan people have mixed feelings about tourism: some have made fortunes but others consider it to be a threat to their culture and traditions. 'Tourism brings degradation', is a typical comment. 'Drugs, pimping, gambling, touting—all these things come around. Police are doing something now, but it is too little and too late.' But the fiercest local reaction is against 'Indian big business', the hotel chains and corporations who are trying to gain control of the state's tourism, ousting the local villagers who now rely on the beach tourists for income.

This local feeling has grown especially strong since Goa finally gained her identity on 31 May 1987 as the 25th state in the Union of India. One aggrieved local remarked, 'The Indians are coming and taking all our land. Over the last ten years, our population has doubled—it's getting all crowded, not only with tourists but with financial sharks from elsewhere in the country buying up all our land. It's not good for the Goan people, you know. We'll be submerged as a minority. Even our culture is being wiped out. After twenty years, you'll find nothing of it.'

Though the main industries of Goa are mining, fishing and tourism, most of her million or so inhabitants still make their living from agriculture: the three main crops being rice, coconut and cashew.

Religion

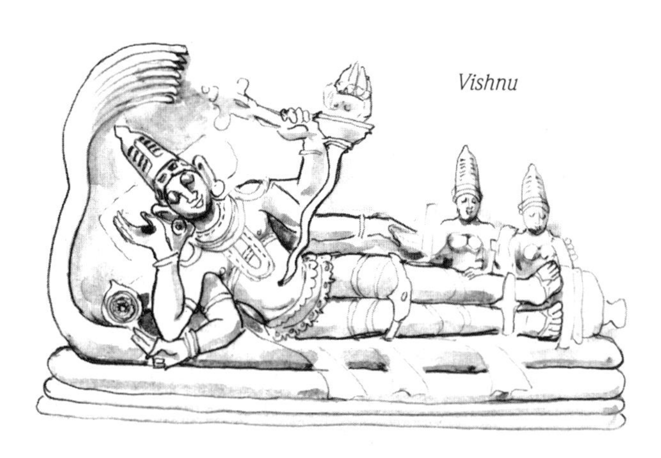

Vishnu

Westerners often have difficulty understanding the importance of religion to the average Indian. It governs every thought, regulates every action and confers a strong sense of identity—the 'dharma', or personal course in life. Religion is everything in Goa, as it is all over India. Goa's multitude of churches and wayside crosses give the impression of a predominantly Catholic society. In fact, only thirty per cent of Goans are Catholic, and most of these live along the coast. Over sixty per cent of Goans are still Hindu, despite the mass forced conversions imposed by the Inquisition between 1580 and 1740 (*see* **History**). The rest are Muslim.

As you move down the coast of Karnataka and Kerala, Buddhism, Jainism and Sikhism, Zoroastrianism (also known as the Parsi Faith), Syrian Orthodox Christianity and even Judaism form a richer patchwork of faiths that, by and large, get along peacefully.

Goa's Main Religions

Hinduism

An ancient repository of Indian spiritual consciousness, Hinduism is the oldest surviving religion in the world and has more adherents than any other religion in Asia. Hinduism went through various periods of prosperity and decline, but demonstrated the most amazing capacity for absorbing and assimilating all competing faiths and was never down for long. One of its earliest scriptures, the *Upanishads* (400–200 BC), stated 'The Great God is One, and the learned call Him by different names'—and it was this aphorism which encapsulated the unique talent for Hindu religious toleration. It never destroyed other beliefs, just synthesised them into its own philosophical system.

Although all forms of worship are acceptable to Hinduism, there are a few basic beliefs which tie the various creeds together. The main three are Samsara, Karma and Dharma. Samsara is the eternity of life in which the soul is believed to pass through a cycle of births and deaths on its way to perfection and to union with the Supreme Being (Brahma). Karma, or the law of cause and effect, is where every thought, word and deed produces a consequent reaction (good or bad) in this or in a subsequent incarnation. Dharma, the code of living, is where every person has a specific role or set of moral duties to perform in life, through which he can break the cycle of rebirth and attain nirvana (heaven).

There are many thousands of gods in the Hindu pantheon. The Aryans were a nomadic people, worshippers of the natural elements. They had a Supreme Being, a central figure who controlled everything in life, but they also had gods to represent all forms of natural energy (sun, moon, wind, water, etc.) and all facets of human life and endeavour (courage, faith, luck, beauty, etc.). The total number of gods was calculated from the estimated population of the known world round the time of the mythical Mahabharata. This was the classic battle between good and evil in which five good brothers, aided by the god Krishna, defeated 100 wicked cousins. It was written down between 200 BC and AD 500, and Indian literature is full of references to it. Over the centuries, many stories and legends grew up round the various gods and goddesses. The main group—the Puranas (AD 500–1500)—became the base of all art in India. Most sculptures and paintings told a 'purana' story and, through such legends and parables, Hindu morals, customs, manners and traditions slowly became crystallized. It was the only way in which the common people received any social education, for the Brahmin priest caste had exclusive access to the ancient Vedic scriptures and holy books and never transferred this knowledge to the masses, except in such symbolic form.

The one supreme God of Hinduism, Parabrahma, has three physical manifestations—Brahma the Creator, Vishnu the Preserver and Shiva the Destroyer. Representing the three basic processes in human life (birth, life and death), this main trinity rules over all the lesser gods. All three deities are normally depicted with four arms, but Brahma also has four heads to show his omniscient wisdom. Unlike the other two, however, very few temples have been built for him. Each god has a 'carrier', an animal or bird who transports him about.

Vishnu is often seen sitting on an eagle with human features called a Garuda. He has visited earth in 9 incarnations (avatars) and is due to pay one last visit, as the horse-headed Kalki. He has already appeared as a fish, a tortoise, a boar, a half-man, a beggar-dwarf and in human form carrying an axe. On his seventh call, he came as Rama with an impossible mission to destroy the demon king Ravana of Lanka (Ceylon). The dramatic story of his success, aided and abetted by the faithful monkey-god Hanuman, became one of the world's greatest epics, the *Ramayana* (350 BC–AD 250). Vishnu made his eighth appearance as Krishna, the dark-skinned boy of the Mathura milkmaids, whom he married 'en masse' after releasing them from the demon king Naraka. A good start for any religious debate with a Hindu is to ask him what he makes of Krishna having 16,000 girlfriends. The ninth incarnation of Vishnu, an imaginative ploy to reabsorb Buddhism back into the Hindu religion, is supposed to have been the Buddha himself.

Shiva's main symbol is the cobra, the virulent snake of death and destruction, though he generally rides out on the bull Nandi. His creative/sexual function is symbolised by the stone lingam. He is often shown with a third eye (sometimes used as a death-ray) and is believed to spend a lot of time in his Himalayan mountain home smoking the holy weed (ganja). When roused, Shiva has a very nasty temper. First he chopped off Brahma's fifth head, and had to wander round as a beggar until the severed skull unstuck itself from his palm. Then he lopped off the head of his younger son, Ganesh, for refusing to let him visit his wife Parvati while she was having a bath. Repenting of his error, Shiva looked round for a new head for his offspring, and came up with one of an elephant. Thus 'lucky' Ganesh, god of good fortune (and divine remover of obstacles) was born. His animal vehicle is the bandicoot, or rat.

Each of the Hindu trinity has a consort, representing the feminine side of their energy. Brahma is married to Saraswati, the goddess of learning, and her vehicle is the swan. Vishnu's consort is the beautiful Lakshmi (Laxmi), goddess of wealth and prosperity. Shiva started out with Sati (who burnt herself to death—the original 'sati' victim), then acquired Parvati, symbol of cosmic energy in the form of Shakti, the World Mother. She is also a symbol (in her dark aspect) of destruction in the form of either Kali, wearing a wreath of skulls, or Durga the terrible, riding a tiger and waving weapons from 10 hands. In addition to Ganesh, Parvati had one other son by Shiva, the six-headed God of War, Kartikkeya (Murugan in south India or Subramanhya).

The good-humoured, indulgent, even playful attitude of many Hindus to their gods is something that mystifies many Westerners, used to religion as rather a solemn business. But while Hinduism is a strict faith, with many rituals, ceremonies and practices geared towards keeping the individual on the general straight and narrow, it has a great inbuilt sense of fun and spectacle. This is especially true on a social level, where births, marriages and even deaths are all an occasion for colourful, noisy bands and processions, complete with caparisoned elephants, performing monkeys, lots of firecrackers and entertainments, and (of course) plentiful free food. It's all a perfect reflection of, and a tribute to, a pantheon of gods who may be gaudy, boisterous and flamboyant but never dull.

Christianity: Catholicism and the Syrian Orthodox Church

There have been Christians in India since St Thomas, one of Christ's Disciples (the doubter, who put his fingers into the still-fresh nail-wounds of the risen Christ before he would believe that He had, in fact, come back from the dead), arrived in Kerala in AD 54. Thomas stayed in south India until his accidental death from a hunter's arrow in a forest near modern Madras in Tamil Nadu, and is believed to be buried near the great San Thom Cathedral just to the south of the city.

Thomas' Indian branch of the Syrian Orthodox Church is the second oldest Christian Church in the world, after that in ancient Palestine, predating both the Coptic (Ethiopian) and Roman churches. During the mid 4th and 8th centuries, two waves of Christian immigrants arrived from the Middle East and a substantial community of 'Syrian Christians' grew up in Kerala.

Later still, in the 16th century, Catholic and Protestant missionaries made a number of converts from various Portuguese, Dutch and English settlements. In the Indian community they concentrated mainly on areas where large numbers of labourers were gathered, such as tea gardens and oil fields, and on the tribal areas of Bihar and north-east India, where they experienced considerable success. The lower castes were naturally more susceptible to conversion as a means of escape from their unchangeably low status in the Hindu caste system.

However, only in Goa, where the forced conversions of the Inquisition and milder activities of the Jesuits left a sizeable Catholic community of relatively influential men (*see* **History**), were the efforts of the missionaries long lasting; the Syrian Orthodox Church in Kerala evolved out of an Indian, rather than a European tradition. Still, travellers will find Indian Christians to he high-profile, as Christian Goans and Keralans will often approach Westerners as 'brothers in faith' and strike up a conversation purely on the basis of an assumed common faith—yet another indication of how important religion is to the average Indian.

Other Religions of the Malabar Coast

Jainism

Jainism was the first major sect to break away from Hinduism and was founded around 500 BC by Vardhamana Mahavira. He was the last of the 24 Jain saints or Tirthankars and was an older contemporary of the Buddha. The schism from Hinduism came from his belief that there was no Supreme Creator of the universe but that it was infinite and eternal. Jain monks are noted for their great asceticism. They have a strict doctrine of *ahimsa* (non-violence to any living creature) and carry brooms to sweep the ground before them clear of any insects and wear a muslin mask to prevent them swallowing any flying parasites. Some even go naked or 'sky-clad' in their rejection of wordly things. There is little or no Jainism in Goa, but temples do occur on the Karnatic coast to the south.

Buddhism

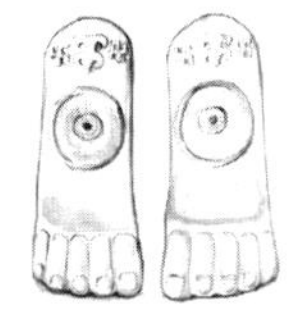

Buddhism was the second reformist offshoot of Hinduism. It was founded by Siddhartha (Shakyamuni) Gautama (during the 5th century BC), a northern Indian prince who, preoccupied by the human problems of old age, sickness and death, forsook riches to embark on a long quest for Truth. After years of rigorous ascetic practice he attained enlightenment at Bodhgaya, and for the final 45 years of his life he taught that every living being could aspire to enlightenment in this lifetime, without awaiting better circumstances in a future incarnation. His central doctrine, whereby enlightenment could be achieved and the cycle of rebirth extinguished, was the eightfold path of the 'middle way'. This put the case for moderation in all things and rejected as harmful the rules, regulations and general extremism of Hinduism and Jainism.

Islam

Goa's initial fortune came from trade with Muslim Arabia. The most recent and successful Asian religion, it was founded by the prophet Mohammed in the early 7th century AD. The Muslim canon, the Koran, is a collection of apocalyptic messages delivered to Mohammed by Allah (God). A keynote of the faith was its militancy, its evangelical zeal to spread the good word—by the sword, if necessary. Starting in Arabia, Islam extended its influence east for several centuries and came to India in the 11th century AD.

Sikhism, Zoroastrianism, Judaism

South India also has a minority population of **Sikhs** who follow a synthesis of Hindu and Islam. The Sikhs are opposed to the caste system, condone the killing of animals for food and believe in one god. They are instantly distinguishable by their *kesa* or unshorn hair (normally wrapped under a turban), and dominate the army and the transport and light engineering industries.

There are also a few Parsis who follow **Zoroastrianism**, founded by the prophet Zoroaster (Zarathustra) in Persia around 800 BC. They fled to India after Muslim persecutions and keep a sacred flame burning in all their temples as a symbol of God. They do not defile the elements by burying or cremating their dead, but expose them atop the 'Towers of Silence' in Bombay to be devoured by kites. The Parsis have a talent for commerce, for example the Tatas, a Parsi family, run the Taj Group of Hotels.

In Cochin in Kerala there is a small population of **Jews**, resident there since the 6th century BC. They were a highly influential community in their time and the Cochin synagogue is the oldest in the Commonwealth, but at present there are only about 28 Cochin Jews remaining, most of whom are in their 70s.

The 13th-century Shri Mahadeva Temple, Tamdi Surla

Architecture

Goa's main architectural legacy consists of the churches, houses, villas and forts built by the Portuguese between the 16th and 19th centuries. The Portuguese created an architectural enclave unique in India, borrowing from indigenous styles to produce buildings that are both beautiful and suited to the climate.

Early Hindu Architecture

Unfortunately, the Portuguese destroyed as much as they created, making it easy to forget that Goa has a native architectural tradition that long predates the arrival of the Portuguese. During the high medieval period (roughly the 12th century), Goa and the whole Malabar Coast saw a period of sumptuous palace and temple building, financed by a sudden expansion of trade with Arabia and the Far East. But modern Goa has only a few small temples from this period, hidden among the forests of the eastern *talukas* where the Muslim invaders of the 14th century and after them the Portuguese—both zealous in their desire to wipe out Hindu 'idolatry'—could not reach them.

The only temple of any size left from this period is the **Shri Mahadeva Temple** at Tamdi Surla in Sanguem *taluka*, built by the Kadambas (*see* **History**). Constructed from the local black basalt in the 13th century, Shri Mahadeva is in the same Deccan style as the larger Chalukyan dynasty complexes of Halebid and Belur, situated just over the eastern mountains in Karnataka. The Deccan style tends to be low, almost squat, with a compact tower known as a *shikara*. Ornate carvings cover the whole building, with lotus motifs on the ceiling, smooth rounded pillars with bulging centres (known as *Kushan*) and stone lattice-work in the cool interior. There are one or two smaller Kadamba temples in Sanguem, but only the Shri Mahadeva is worth making the long bus-ride up through the hills to see.

Muslim Architecture

The Muslim armies of Bijapur which overran eastern Goa in the late 14th century razed almost every temple and palace they found, and built their own places of government and worship. In their turn, the Muslim buildings were almost all destroyed by Christians. Only one of each type of building survived the Portuguese conquest: the Secretariat building in Panjim and the Safa Mosque in Ponda *taluka*. The Secretariat, built on the waterfront by the modern steamer jetty and used as a summer palace, differed little from the older Hindu style of Malabar palace building. A modest but handsome construction of whitewashed walls, cool high-ceilinged interiors and a tiered roof of red Mangalore tiles, it is designed to provide shade and to catch the breezes blowing in off the Mandovi estuary. The Safa Mosque in Ponda is also a modest affair. Built of laterite, its walls are carved with wide Saracenic arches of a style that was developed in Bijapur on the Deccan Plateau, and the whole is topped with a simple pitched roof. Steps lead down to a large tank, now partly ruined.

The Portuguese Period

Forts

The Portuguese trading empire was safeguarded by its coastal forts. Almost all of them proved effective against cannon and siege, being built, with very few exceptions, with freshwater springs inside the walls and thick walls that expanded outwards at the base, so that cannon balls rolled off on impact. Goa never fell by storm—not even during the Maratha wars of the late 17th century. Almost all the forts occupy natural headlands and have pointed landward bastions linked by wide ramparts along which large cannons could be manoeuvred. Because of the thickness of their bases, the walls and bastions were almost impossible to undermine and their headland locations allowed the Portuguese artillery to dominate both the water and landward approaches.

If you plan to visit the Goan forts, why not stay in one? Those travelling in style can try the luxuriously developed **Fort Aguada** just north of Panjim (*see* p.72), while anyone on a tighter budget should head for **Terekol Fort** in the far north, which has been transformed into a tourist hostel and has its own church inside the defences.

Religious Buildings

Many Renaissance travellers compared Old Goa to Rome, for the sheer splendour of its great cathedrals, basilicas and churches. Detailed descriptions of these buildings are given on pp.67–70; this section details some of the architectural types that mark out the Goan ecclesiastical style.

Almost all Goa's religious buildings are in the local red or black laterite stone and each one sports a wide, ornate whitewashed front topped by twin bell towers and a central pediment and cross, or by a larger pediment and cross with a single bell tower perched on the side. The façades generally rise for three storeys, each one separated by stuccoed cross-beams 'supported' by decorative false pillars, topped with either Doric, Ionian or Corinthian capitals. Goan interiors are often no less ornate, with rounded vaulting ceilings also 'supported' by tier upon tier of false pillars, creating an illusion of additional height. This effect is seen at its most striking in the Church of St Catejan and the Church of St Francis of Assisi in Old Goa.

Although the most impressive churches are in Old Goa, it is worth dropping into the local parish churches, some of which are surprisingly beautiful. Try to visit the Seminary of Rachol, built in the 1560s. Constructed around a great, cloistered courtyard, the seminary church has a majestic high altar and some exquisite frescoes. The church at Loutolim is another favourite, its front decorated with rising sun motifs, as is the huge Church of the Immaculate Conception, in Panjim, which is approached by series of staircases built into the hill in several overlapping diagonals.

Villas

The Portuguese developed a style of house building that can be called truly Goan, and is easily distinguished from their colonial styles in Africa and the Far East. The most distinctive feature is the roof, which is much more sharply pitched than is usual in colonial architecture. This form of roof building was adopted by the Portuguese from the Kadamba and Muslim houses that they found when they arrived. Goa's monsoons are particularly heavy and prolonged (lasting for almost four months), and a sharp pitch is needed for drainage. Goan roofs are covered with the red Mangalore tiles, used on the Malabar Coast since at least the 13th century. Their distinctive crenellated design gives them an unmistakeably Asian look, and they are arranged in such a way as to allow a greater movement of air than European roofs, which are built for insulation.

Goan villas are usually built on one or two storeys only, around a central courtyard garden and with a wide verandah running around either the whole building or along the front. They generally have a large, sparsely furnished reception room, with wide doorways to let in the breeze and high, pointed windows which look like those of a church but are in fact a survival from the Iberian Moorish style of house building.

Most of these villas are still privately occupied. However, you can obtain permission to view several of the best, including: the very grand, 16th–18th century Menenzes Braganza House at Chandor (*see* p.110), which has a superb collection of period furniture and an interesting library (if you can read Portuguese); the very early 18th-century Miranda House at Loutolim, which has a beautiful tiled verandah and ornate hardwood carving on the doors; and the early 20th-century Albuquerque Mansion at Anjuna, which is now a state museum.

Later Hindu Temples

By the mid-1700s, with the decline of the Inquisition, wealthy local Hindus began to build grand temples again, especially in the inland *taluka* of Ponda, just east of Old Goa. Just as the Portuguese borrowed from local styles in their house building, these later temples adopted European church motifs, resulting in several temples whose design is unique to Goa. False Classical pillars, inspired by the Renaissance churches, appear on the outer façades. And there is a square symmetry to the buildings unusual in indigenous Indian architecture. Domes, found in temples nowhere else in India, rise from the centre of the roofs.

Most of the larger temples bear free-standing lamp towers (resembling tall, solidly built dovecotes), in whose arched enclaves oil lamps were lit during festivals. This is a style borrowed from the Marathas, who overran much of eastern Goa during the 1700s. Try to make time to see the massive Shri Mangesh Temple at Priol, the Shri Shantadurga Temple at Queula and the Shri Mahalsa Temple at Mardol.

Topics

Goa's Sanitary Engineers

Goa's sandy villages, spread out under the shade of tall coconut palms, have no sewage system. Yet you never see any waste lying around, either human or animal. What you do see are a lot of pigs. They're everywhere: great sows farrowing in the lee of the huts; piratical bands of nippy yearlings, squealing away in a score of directions when you surprise them as they root through the garbage behind the beach restaurants; happy couples mating uninhibitedly by the ocean.

Oddly, you never see anyone feeding these hundreds, thousands, tens of thousands of pigs. Only when you stagger to the loo on your first hot morning do you realize who feeds them. The palm-thatch door of the outhouse rattles as you pull it to and settle yourself down to business. Then behind you comes the quiet patter of trotters. Some people looking behind them at this point may glimpse a questing snout snortling through the gap in the back of the thatch where the waste rolls out. Others only hear the happy gruntings that immediately follow the 'flushing' out of the waste with a bucket.

It is therefore most unwise to eat pork in Goa, though unsqueamish devotees claim that it is the sweetest anywhere in the world—especially in the form of the spicy Goan *chourisso* or pork sausage. But do not think of the pigs as disgusting. Goa is a remarkably clean place, given its dense coastal population, and disease gets little chance to breed—all thanks to the pigs. And you couldn't wish for a more charming corps of sanitary engineers, grunting and copulating their way through brief but festive lives on their way to becoming *chourissos*, bringing the wheel full circle.

Beaches

Goa's beaches vary enormously. Those seeking parties, techno music and drugs should head straight for north Baga, Anjuna and Vagator beaches on the coast near Mapusa. Those seeking more of a holiday-resort atmosphere should stay at southern Baga and Calangute, north of Panjim, or Colva and the beaches south of Vasco da Gama (where you should be prepared to share the sands with thousands of Indian tourists at weekends). If you are on a lowish budget and want a quieter beach that isn't too secluded, then head for Palolem or Benaulim in the south. For the same atmosphere but on a high budget, there are the exclusive resort hotels at Dona Paula and Fort Aguada near Panjim, and the slightly cheaper resorts around Cavelossim, south of Colva. For sheer unspoilt tranquility, head straight for Arambol and Terekol in the far north and Betul and Rajabag in the south.

Most travellers like to sample a little of each kind of atmosphere, moving up and down the coast as the mood takes them. It is a good idea to remain flexible in this way. When you arrive, book into a hotel or lodge for a few days only. If you like it, stay; if not, move on until you find that perfect spot that all visitors to Goa seem to find in the end.

The Hippy Techno Trail

South India's resident hippy scene has changed in recent years—particularly with regard to music—with almost all Europeans heavily into techno. And while the old hippy uniform of long hair and loose, brightly patterned clothes is still in evidence, it is rapidly being replaced by the New Age traveller look of shaved heads and dreadlocks (there are even skinny dogs on the beaches to adopt).

The mellow hippy attitude has changed along with the music and the clothes. The all-night techno parties at Goa's Anjuna and Vagator beaches, and now even at Kovalam, are about Ecstasy, acid and money first, peace, love and dope second.

Those who love New-Age hippiedom and its 'smart' techno fashions will find heaven in north Goa, and even the unconverted should find the parties fun. Who wouldn't want to dance all night on a warm tropical beach, whether they liked loud, incessant techno or not? If you want to find a party, head straight for the Shore Bar at Anjuna or the Primrose at Vagator where they will know when the next party is (probably that night), while the Kovalam ones (in Kerala) happen on Lighthouse Beach.

There is still no entrance fee for parties, but once you have covered your transport there and back by motorcycle taxi and bought a few beers and some *chai* and cake between dances, you will find it hard to spend less than Rs200 for the night. If you want to buy drugs, it will cost you considerably more.

On the subject of drugs, a word of warning. The general attitude of *laissez-faire* on the beaches is misleading. If you look the part, it is not uncommon to be spot-searched by police. For some years now, the Goan and Kovalam police have been making money out of on-the-spot-fines and even planting drugs on suspects. If you are caught with any drug, it's straight to jail. You'll generally be given a simple choice: 10 years, or a Rs10–20,000 fine. If you are caught with heroin or its local derivative, 'brown sugar', you may not be given a choice.

The older, slower hippy scene has fled to the far northern beaches of Goa and is still gamely resisting the techno invasion in Kovalam. It has also colonized some new beaches where the facilities are too basic and the life too mellow to attract ravers. The best of these are Arambol, Terekol and Rajabag in Goa; Varkala and Bekal in Kerala and Gokarn and Karwar in Karnataka, where the impact of travellers is still very light and techno has not yet crept in to obliterate the sigh of moonlit ocean.

Ruins of the High Renaissance

It's a sad fact that many travellers never visit Old Goa. Once the easternmost capital of Christendom but abandoned in the 18th century after a succession of cholera epidemics, this city, just east of Panjim, rivalled Rome for splendour. Today Old Goa's power and glory are long gone but the great pompous churches, cathedrals and basilicas still stand, monuments to one of Renaissance Europe's most ruinous imperial endeavours.

In the Basilica of Bom Jesus you can join the never-ending queue of pilgrims come to gaze through the glass casket with the gilded frame at the mottled skull and cast-silver toes of St Francis Xavier (all that is visible of the mummified body in its great swathing shroud), while above you hangs a chain-mail shower of stars wrought on goldsmiths' anvils.

In the Se Cathedral the whitewashed soaring arches are suddenly cool after the burning heat outside. For a moment you are blinded by the shadow, then the frescoes reveal themselves, covering the altarpiece and illuminating the side chapels. The solemn Renaissance faces painted onto the Biblical characters call to mind the first Europeans who landed uncertainly, uncomprehendingly, in this timeless harbour of the East; entering a world of strange diseases, unfathomable beliefs and sensual langour, cut off from the religious wars and flawed chivalry of late medieval Europe. Though they tried to bring that world with them—its glories, as the great buildings show, and its horrors such as the Inquisition—the settlers died in their hundreds. The floor is paved with memorials to them, headed always with the moniker *Sepultura*, below which flourishes a plumed helmet, visor raised, and the family arms.

Behind the cathedral in the soaring, white-stuccoed roof-vaults of the Church of St Catejan, doves flutter out across the silent spaces from nests they have built in the capitals of the Corinthian pillars.

Try to attend Mass just once during your stay; or, if you are staying too far away from Old Goa's churches and cathedrals, settle for second-best and go to one of the countless Renaissance churches that dot the provincial towns and villages. Of particular beauty are the high-roofed Church of the Immaculate Conception in Panjim, Our Lady of Miracles in Mapusa, Our Lady of Help in Cavelossim and Our Lady of Compassion on Diwar Island in the Mandovi River near Old Goa. Amid the incense and candles you can glimpse the sombre Renaissance sharper than in Europe, thrown into relief against the chaotic canvas of modern India.

Portuguese? What Portuguese?

The multitude of Baroque churches, European-style villas and Portuguese names make it clear that this was once a Lusitanian colony. What is not clear, however, is why you don't see any Portuguese people. This seems to rather contradict Goa's obvious heritage, especially when you consider that both the colonists and home government actively encouraged intermarriage with the locals (at least with those who converted to Christianity). So what happened to Goa's Portuguese?

After about 1750 the waves of immigration from the Old Country that had supplied Goa with colonists were halted by the great cholera epidemics of the late 18th and early 19th centuries. The generations that followed were descendants of the first mixed marriages. They inherited the names of the old families, their religion and many of their customs but applied them to a culture that had become specifically Goan rather than Portuguese. Added to this, many early converts to Christianity were given Portuguese names, which they keep to this day, without ever marrying into European families.

Apart from a small minority of plantation owners who abandoned the colony at Independence in 1961 (or were dispossessed), the only full-blooded Portuguese to live in Goa after the mid-19th century were civil servants, engineers, governors and the like. These men came to India only for a specific term, finally retiring back to Portugal. Few Goans today even understand Portuguese. The outer trappings of the old colonial culture are everywhere but the colonists themselves are long gone.

On the Beach

'Hello Baby!' cried a voice. Two teenage Indian boys, lean silhouettes, were walking along the beach. Catching sight of my long hair, they had mistaken me for a girl. They flinched with embarrassment when I looked up—all five-day stubble and knowing grin—but recovered in a moment. 'We meant Baba,' said the taller one. *Baba* means 'uncle' in Hindi and is a universal Indian greeting for any adult male. 'I don't believe you,' I replied. 'Anyway, you shouldn't address women as "Baby", it's rude.'

The two boys took this as an invitation to sit down. 'True?' asked the tall one again, obviously not believing me since he had seen countless American films where the actors said 'Baby' and no offence was taken. He crossed his legs underneath him comfortably. 'That your guitar?' asked the smaller one. 'Can I try?' I held out the instrument to him, expecting a ham-fisted attempt at strumming.

'What would you like to hear?' asked the youth. Without waiting for a reply, he applied expert fingers to the fretboard and began to pick out a slow, precise tune of great loveliness. I sat transfixed, along with the taller youth, until the melody was broken by shouts from further down the beach.

A score of yards away from us five fishermen wearing the thinnest of loincloths were jogging down to the shore. A long, dark, wooden boat was cutting through the waves towards the beach. The five lean men ran into the surf and grabbed the prow, dragging the boat from the water as easily as if it was made of balsa rather than solid tropical hardwood. The crew sprang out and together the nine of them hauled it almost fully onto the beach. Then one man took hold of a rope that stretched taut from the stern of the boat into the water. At a shout from him the others also took the rope and, hand over hand, began hauling in the net, heavy with fish. Gulls and crows wheeled above them and the sun, disappearing below the edge of the ocean horizon, dyed the waves red.

Head Waggling

As a vital hint on communication I must mention the head-waggle. Most travellers realize within a few days that Indians do not nod when they mean 'yes' but waggle their heads from side to side in a motion that is dangerously similar to the head-shake for 'no'—which *is* used in India.

If you pick up the head-waggling habit you will often find yourself much better understood. This is not hard to do as the waggle is definitely contagious and most travellers to India find themselves doing it on their return to their 'native place', to the consternation of friends and family.

There are different kinds of head-waggle, however. The brisk, business-like head-waggle, with the head slightly bouncing at the end of each side-waggle denotes a definite 'yes', or 'I understand'. If you want to be more ambiguous slow the waggle down and put in a slightly longer bounce at the end of each side-waggle—this denotes that you are affirmatively disposed but not necessarily fully committed. Lastly, there is a high-speed head-waggle accompanied by a cheeky grin which serves both as an admission of having done wrong but also of having got away with it. If a rickshaw driver uses it when you ask about a fare, you know he's cheating you. Similarly, if you stick to your price and use the same head-waggle, your adversary will know that you know that he's cheating you and are good-humouredly holding your ground and will probably yield to a lower price with less argument and bad feeling.

Flora and Fauna

Goa still has a surprising amount of wild land. Only the coastline is densely populated. About a quarter of the state is still covered by hardwoods. Travel by bus between the northern and southern beaches and you will cross areas of dense hardwood forest. In the eastern *talukas*, the forest takes over almost completely, rising into the mountain range known as the Western Ghats which marks the Goa/Karnataka state border.

Conservation

Conservation groups, particularly the World Wide Fund for Nature (WWF), are very active in Goa. The state has three designated wildife reserves—Bondla, Bhagwan Mahavir and Cotigao Wildlife Sanctuaries—and some large areas of Reserved Forest (protected forest). There have also been various afforestation projects in the past fifteen years, including a successful attempt to turn some 6000 acres of old mining dumps back into forest. Spotted deer, wild boar and leopard have since moved back to the area.

Goa is also known to ornithologists all over the world. The state has two wetland bird sanctuaries and indigenous forest species, Chorao and Karmali Lake, which attract tens of thousands of migrant waders every year. These sanctuaries are mostly composed of coastal mangrove swamps, a habitat that has been disappearing from India's southwestern Malabar Coast over the past twenty or thirty years as farmers reclaim the mud-flats for agricultural land. There are now some efforts to reverse this process in Goa, where only 4000 acres of mangrove have survived intact; since 1985 the Forestry Department has replanted four million seedlings around the coastal river mouths.

For full details of the sanctuaries, *see* pp.117–20. The following is a list of the state's principal plant and animal species.

Flora

In Goa's eastern *takula* rise the foothills of the Western Ghats, their steep slopes covered with hardwood. Large trees such as wild mango, teak, rosewood, sandalwood, frankincense, camphor, peepul and flame-of-the-forest tower over an underbrush of wild cardamom and thorn, while wild pepper vines wind up the great tree-trunks towards the canopy. On the higher slopes the forest stays green all year but in the lower foothills most of the trees lose their leaves during the hot season, which lasts from February to late June or early July.

Flowers are always abundant in Goa. Many of those you see on the coast are exotics such as the omnipresent bougainvillaea, passion-flower and various types of clematis and morning-glory. Look out for indigenous lotus and water hyacinths in lakes and temple tanks. In some of the forest wildlife sanctuaries you may see rare species of orchids in November or December—the months immediately after the monsoons when the vegetation is at its most vibrant.

Mammals

Goa's three wildlife sanctuaries harbour most of the south Indian species. Tiger pass through the area fairly regularly but the shy, nocturnal leopard is much more common. There is a small resident wild elephant herd which moves between Bondla and Bhagwan Mahavir sanctuaries.

Other game present throughout the mountains includes sloth bear (almost never seen); *dhole* or wild dog, a reddish-coloured pack canid about the size of a coyote and also seldom seen; the huge *gaur* or Indian bison, which you are almost certain to see at Bondla; *chital* or spotted deer; the larger *sambar* deer (south India's equivalent of the British red deer); the small muntjac, or barking deer; the even smaller *chevrotain* or mouse deer; and occasionally the *chousingha*, a minute four-horned antelope that exists only in southern India. Wild boar are common throughout the forests. Apart from leopard, wild cats include jungle cat, genets and civets. There are various monkey species, with common *langur* and bonnet macaque being the most common. Faunal oddities include the *pangolin*, a scaly anteater which looks very similar to an armadillo and the slow *loris*, a tiny creature like a cross between a sloth and a bushbaby that is in fact a kind of miniature lemur. Both the *pangolin* and *loris* are nocturnal and seldom seen.

Birds

Ornithologists will be pleasantly surprised by Goa; the latest World Wide Fund for Nature checklist of Goa's bird species numbers just under 350—an impressive number for such a small geographical area. The state has two bird sanctuaries: the wetlands of Chorao (*see* p.120) and Karmali Lake (*see* p.120), which provide a dazzling spectacle from November to March when thousands of storks, waders and other waterfowl species fly in from the north. In the upland forests you can expect to see the following colourful species year-round: paradise flycatcher, racket-tailed drongo, peacock, several hornbill species, rufous woodpecker, rosy minivet, ruby-throated yellow bulbul, green pigeon, emerald dove, several parakeet species, Indian roller, green bee-eater, trogon, rosy starling, several species of sunbird, black-headed oriole, tree pie, Indian pitta and white-throated fantail flycatcher. In addition to these spectacular avids there are large raptors such as the serpent eagle, crested serpent eagle, white-bellied fish-eagle (not to be confused with the brahmini kite, common on the coast, which looks like a white-headed fish eagle), south Indian crested goshawk, osprey and a small aerobatic similar to a kestrel called a shaheen falcon. If you stay on the beach, all you are likely to see are the brown pariah kites that live everywhere in India, their confederates the crows, and perhaps kingfishers at the river mouths.

Reptiles

Goa has many species of reptile but most tourists will only see small lizards and skinks and, of course, geckos in their rooms. The great Indian snakes—reticulated python and king cobra, both of which can grow to over five metres—are confined to the wildest upland forests. There are numerous harmless varieties, including large water-snakes and the big dark-brown rat-snake. However, the three commonest Indian venomous snakes do occur. These are: Indian cobra; the small krait, a blue-black viper with narrow white crosses that can strike in the dark using scent as a guide; the chain-patterned Russel's viper and the triangular-headed saw-scaled viper, which is all too easy to step on on forest and mountain paths. You are very unlikely to encounter any snake on the well populated coast because snakes don't like disturbance, but its sensible to wear boots if you are going to walk in the wooded gardens of big hotels and to swish a stick through the undergrowth, especially at night, as tourists do occasionally get bitten. If it happens to you, almost all regional hospitals carry serums for these four snake species.

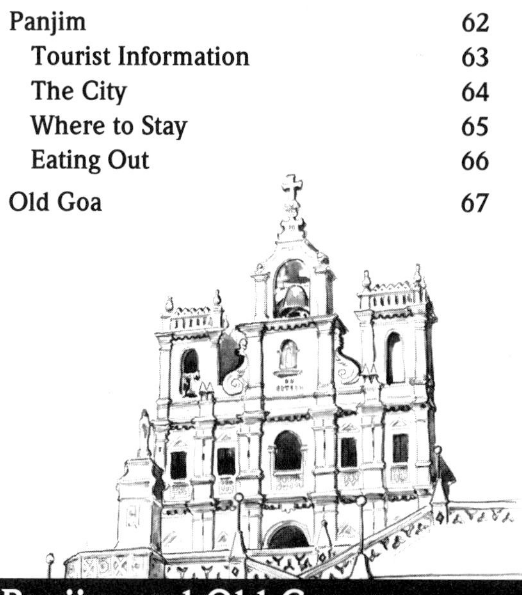

Panjim and Old Goa

Church of the Immaculate Conception, Panjim

Panjim

Until it replaced Old Goa as capital of Portuguese India in 1843, Panjim or Panaji ('Land which does not get Flooded') was little more than a fishing village. Today, it is one of India's smallest and most pleasant capitals and also one of the least 'Indian'. Its Portuguese colonial heritage has survived more or less intact. White-washed, red-tiled houses and narrow, winding avenues, small cafés, bars and tavernas make up the 'old town' on the hill above the Mandovi estuary.

Panjim is the obvious base from which to explore the rest of Goa, not simply because most tourist facilities (Indian Airlines, banks, the post office and jetty) are concentrated here, but also for the two Goa sightseeing tours running from Panjim's tourist office—useful both for checking out accommodation on the major beaches and for getting to some of the inland sights.

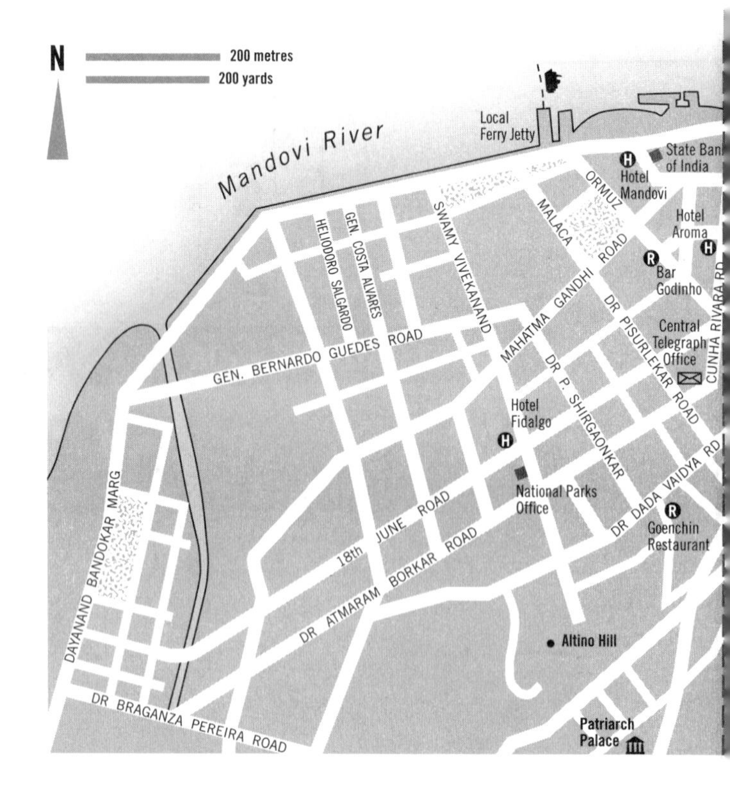

The **Goan Tourist Office** is at the Tourist Home, Patto Bridge, below Panjim bus stand, ✆ (0832) 225715 (open 9.30–1.15 and 2–5.45, Mon–Fri. Excellent information, helpful staff and a trained guide service for about Rs350 per day. They have regular launch cruises with a cultural programme (departures daily at 6pm and 7.15pm, a 1-hour trip costs Rs50). Tourist taxis and luxury mini-coaches are also for hire. The **Goa Tourism Development Corporation** (**GTDC**), Trionora Apartments, ✆ (0832) 226515, run various tours which are available from the Tourist Hostel.

There are Government of India tourist information counters at the Municipal Building, Church Square, ✆ (0832) 223412, Panjim bus stand, ✆ (0832) 225620, and at Diabolim airport.

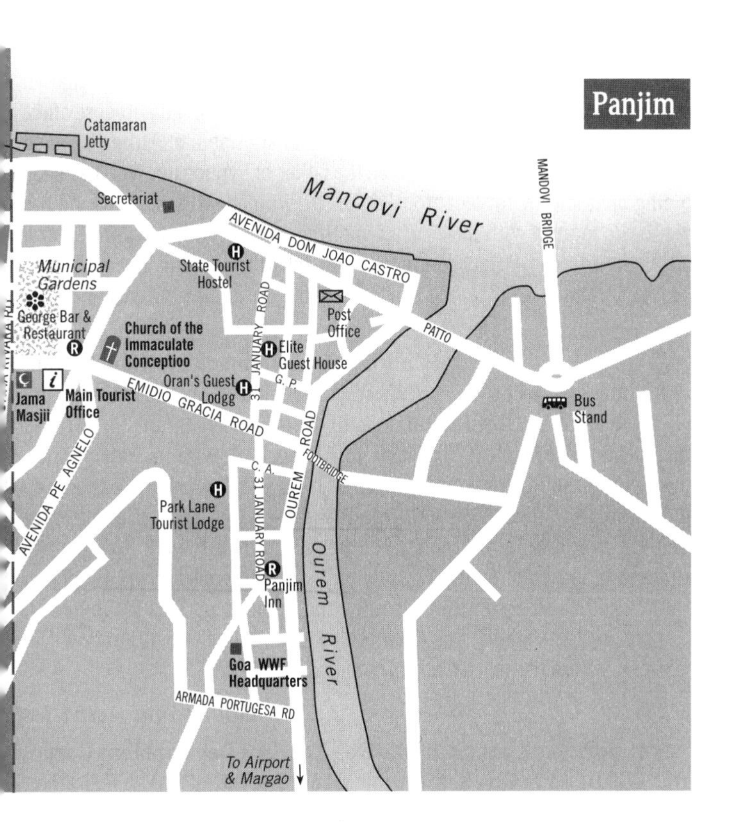

The **State Bank of India** is just up from the Tourist Hostel (open 10–2 Mon–Fri, and 10–12 Sat, closed Sun). The **Foreigners' Registration Office** is at the Police Headquarters in Panjim, © (0832) 45360.

Note that most **shops** are closed on Sundays. The **post office** is midway between Tourist Hostel and Patto Bridge.

Indian Airlines, at Dempo House, D. Bandodkar Marg, © (0832) 223826, lays on regular Rs30 buses to the airport. Other domestic airlines are handled by **Jet Air**, © (0832) 223891 and the **National Travel Service**, © (0832) 223324. **Air India** is at Hotel Fidalgo, 18th June Road, © (0832) 224081.

The City

Panjim is best enjoyed at leisure. The townsfolk keep alive the Mediterranean tradition of relaxing evening promenades and unhurried drinks in jolly tavernas. During the day you can visit its few sights in a couple of hours on foot or by auto-rickshaw. Start in the main thoroughfare, Dayanand Bandodkar Road, at the **Tourist Hostel**. Opposite, you'll see the busy little **steamer wharf**, which services the Bombay catamaran and runs evening river cruises. Strolling right, you'll pass the small sub-post office (with its distinctive striped postbox), then the extraordinary statue of **Abbe Faria**, an 18th-century Goan churchman, believed to be the father of hypnotism, who has been carved, looming demonically (or lecherously?) over a woman who, it seems, he has just knocked to the ground with his crucifix and transfixed with his hypnotic stare. Opposite this is the **Idalcao Palace** or **Secretariat building** (originally built by the Adil Shah of Bijapur and until 1759 the residence of the Portuguese viceroys).

Turning left here, you'll soon find yourself in scruffy Church Square (Communicada Street), with its beautiful white **Church of the Immaculate Conception**, built in 1600, sitting on the hill above. A short walk behind this is the 18th-century **Jama Masjid** mosque and the **Mahalakshmi Temple**, an interesting Hindu shrine. Next, make the 20-minute ascent up to **Altino Hill**, with its stately **Patriarch Palace** (where the Pope stayed during his 1986 Goan tour) and panoramic views over Panjim's red-tiled roofs and tree-shaded squares, with the glittering Mandovi spilling over into the Arabian Sea beyond. On the walk down, note Altino's bungalows and colonnaded houses, with their flower-decked windows, stray cats, and caged canaries on the balconies and verandahs. This is the oldest, most Latin, quarter of town and runs from the terraced hillock of Altino down to 31 January Street, where the town's cheaper tourist lodges are.

Sports and Activities

River cruises: these are run by the **Goa Tourism Development Corporation** (**GTDC**) and **Goa Sea Travels Agency** at the jetty. The Full Moon

Cruise is best, 7.30–9.30pm, with lively Portuguese folk dances on deck, meals provided and an unforgettable moon rising above the night horizon like a giant tarnished penny.

Cinema: For English-language films, look in the Tourist Hostel lobby.

Swimming: you can find safe clean water at Panjim's two local beaches, Miramar (2 miles away) and Dona Paula (5 miles away), both well connected by a regular local bus service.

Football: the Portuguese left their passion for soccer in Goa, just as the British left theirs for cricket in the rest of the country. Panjim's big local sport can be seen at the stadium every Sunday afternoon (4pm kick-off).

Panjim ✆ (0832–)

Where to Stay

expensive

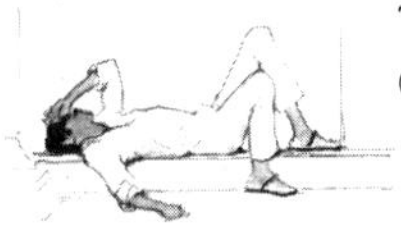

The only luxury-style option is the **Cicade de Goa**, ✆ 221133, ℻ 243303, a resort at Dona Paula with attractive rooms, marvellous water sports and superior Goan/Mughlai cuisine. A popular place for family holidays is the **Prainha Cottages by the Sea** at Dona Paula, ✆ 224162/225917, ℻ 223433/80218, with fully air-conditioned rooms.

In Panjim itself, the top place is **Hotel Fidalgo**, 18th June Road, ✆ 226291/9 or 223330/2, ℻ 225061, with fawning flunkeys, central air-conditioning and a swimming pool. Rather more relaxing is **Hotel Mandovi**, D.B. Bandodkar Road, ✆ 226270/4 or 224405/9, ℻ 225451, offering nice air-conditioned rooms with river views and staff who leave you alone when you want to be left. The 2-star **Hotel Nova Goa**, Dr Atmaram Borkar Road, ✆ 226231/9, has air-conditioning, restaurant and snack bar.

moderate

One of Goa's most stylish hotels is the **Panjim Inn**, on 31 January Street, ✆ 226523, ℻ 228136. An old understated Portuguese villa, it has a beautiful verandah and rooms with grand old mahogany beds, some of them four-posters, hung with mosquito netting. The owner is a bit of an art connoisseur and has hung the old halls with abstracts. These sit eclectically next to trophy heads of *sambar* deer shot in the mountains. The food is very good traditional Goan fare and there is a free airport pick-up service for guests.

inexpensive

The **Hotel Aroma**, on Cunha Rivara Road, © 223984, is a well-located place with clean rooms and pleasant air-conditioned restaurant opposite the Municipal Gardens. The state-run **Tourist Hostel,** © 225715/227972, faces the river near the Secretariat. It is exceedingly popular (often booked out weeks ahead), has a good open-air restaurant, useful shopping complex and spacious rooms, some with balconies and good river views. If the hostel is full, Panjim has some other decent options: try the **Mayfair Hotel**, Dr Dada Vaidya Road, © 225772, 226174/5, 225952 or 225773; the **Hotel Neptune** on Malaca Road, © 222601; the **Hotel Samrat**, also on Dada Vaidya Road, © 223318/9 or 224546/7/8; or the **Hotel Sunrise**, © 223960, opposite the Sheela Building on 18th June Road.

cheap

Anything in this category is bound to be rough: Panjim's hotel owners are used to the idea that tourists have money and seldom offer good value for cheap rooms. You should certainly have your own mosquito net and sheet. However, on 31 January Street you can find several cheap lodges that aren't too awful. The best is the **Hotel Venite**, © 225537/227455. If that's full, walk along the street and try the **Poonam Lodge**, **Orav's Guest House**, **Lilia Dias Guest House**, **Elite Lodge** or **Delux Lodge** (although the last two are both pretty ropey).

Other options in town include the **Safari Hotel** opposite the Municipal Gardens on Cunha Rivara Road, © 226475/226054, the **Mandovi Guest House**, © 226852/223928, behind the Tourist Hostel, overlooking the boat jetty and **Frank's Inn** on the second floor of the Orion Building on the Rua Menezes Braganza.

Eating Out

Avanti, near Patto Bridge, is probably Panjim's favourite eating spot, with a popular air-conditioned lounge. Get your spicy Goan sausage, prawn curry and rice here; no dish is more than Rs25. Don't show up between 1 and 2pm, when it's packed with local diners. The **Panjim Inn** on 31 January Street serves traditional Goan dishes like spicy chicken and sole in wine—not cheap but good value and served on the verandah of this old Portuguese villa.

Despite rather risky food, **O'Coqueiro**, at Alto Parvorim (just outside Panjim on the Mapusa road), is still the nearest thing to non-hippy nightlife in Goa, according to many locals. Prices are cheap and the prawn balchao is superb. Despite poor service, **Hotel Mandovi** is still capable of producing excellent Goan and Portuguese cuisine, and there's often a live band. Of Panjim's numerous bars and grills, try **Casa Olympia**, opposite the gardens in Communicada Square. It's owned by a real old pirate and is a great place to meet the local people.

Other typically Goan eating places are **Bar Godinho**, the main backpackers' hangout near the National Theatre in Cinema Square, **Bar George** on Communicada Square and the slightly more expensive **City Bar and Restaurant**. On Dr Cunha Gonsalves Road, the **Hotel Venite** has balcony tables where you can eat good grilled fish and chips.

For lighter food, cross the street from Godinho's and go round the corner to the **Hanuman Cold Drink House**, which serves excellent shakes, ices and *lassis*. Nearby **Kamat Hotel**, at the top of Municipal Gardens, does delicious and cheap vegetarian food, while **Chit-Chat** at the Tourist Hostel has 'ravishing tandooris', and is a pleasant place to sit out in the evenings.

Panjim has a superb, but expensive, Chinese restaurant with a relaxed atmosphere: **The Riverdeck**, near the jetty and on the waterfront. The **Mandan** vegetarian restaurant, attached to the Hotel Rajdhani on Dr Atmaran Borker Road is air-conditioned and serves excellent Indian and Chinese food in spotless surroundings.

Old Goa

Five and a half miles from Panjim, Old Goa is described by many as a cathedral 'ghost town'. This is misleading: true, the huge basilicas (which rival anything in Europe for size and splendour), now stand alone amid tended lawns, but in fact houses still dot the palm forest behind and Old Goa still 'lives', despite having been abandoned by the Portuguese early last century after a succession of plagues.

In the High Renaissance heyday of Goa's prosperity, the priests of Rome were the real rulers, not the Portuguese conquistadors, and the religious arrogance of the 17th-century Catholic Church is reflected in the grandiose complex of churches, monasteries and convents. The Portuguese arrived here in 1510, bearing a sword in one hand, a crucifix in the other and within 150 years, Goa Velha, as Old Goa was then called, became a city of great splendour and power, dominated by the huge ecclesiastical buildings which replaced the old mosques and temples of former Muslim and Hindu rulers. But with the buildings came great plagues (1543, 1635 and 1735), which killed 80 per cent of the population. In 1835 Old Goa was abandoned and the administrative capital transferred to Panjim. Today, only the hulks of the huge convents and churches (some half-ruined) and the tourists that beetle between them over the sparkling lawns, testify to Old Goa's past splendour.

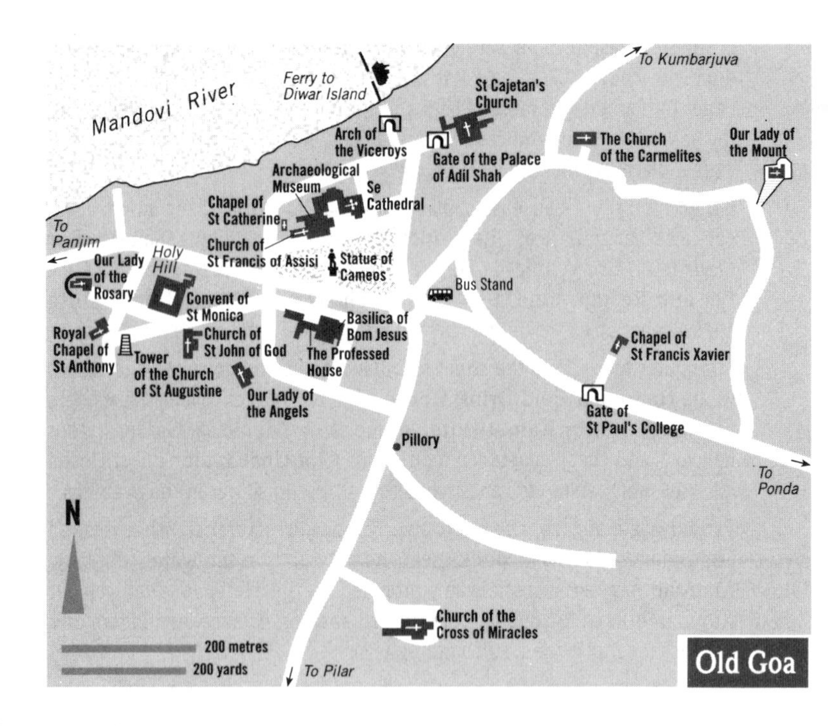

At present, only six of the town's original 14 churches remain in good condition, their red laterite structures eroded by centuries of wind and rain. They're a complete contrast to Hindu temples and shrines, though some find these haughty Catholic structures uncomfortably unlike India, much more reminiscent of Lisbon or Rome. If returning for a longer look, come in by local bus from either Panjim (20 minutes) or Margao (40 minutes). Old Goa really should be appreciated at leisure—one can spend hours wandering round the vast, deserted cloisters and corridors of these decaying old buildings. The Archaeological Survey of India has published an excellent 52-page guide, *Old Goa*, which is available locally and at their New Delhi office.

The **Basilica of Bom Jesus** (*open daily, 9–6.30; Mass at 7am and 8am weekdays, 8am and 9.15am Sun; no photography allowed*), is Goa's most popular and famous church (now a World Heritage Site). Built between 1594 and 1604, the rather dim interior is enlivened by the gilded Baroque high altar, with elaborate screens and spiral columns and by the huge, gaudy statue of Ignatius Loyola, the founder of the Jesuit order. To the right of the altar is the Basilica's big attraction—the silver casket enshrining the mummified **remains of St Francis Xavier**, Goa's patron saint, who spent his life spreading Christianity among the Portuguese colonies. Murals of events from the saint's life run round the walls of the Italian-marble sarcophagus enclosing the casket. One of the most well-travelled corpses in history, Xavier was taken all over the place after his death in China in 1552 and only came to rest here in 1613. During his posthumous travels, one of his toes was bitten off in 1554 by a Portuguese hunter of holy relics, who apparently kept the member hidden in his mouth until his return to Europe. Later, as the grisly process of dismemberment continued, he lost a hand to the Japanese Jesuits (1619), had various sections of intestine removed, and suffered a broken neck after being stuffed in an undersized grave. Today, what's left of his corpse is remarkably well preserved. If you don't believe it, you can peer at Xavier's bald, mottled head—illuminated within the casket by a naked bulb—or, for a donation, view his silver-encased toes. Every 10 years, the shrivelled cadaver is given a public veneration (the next occasion will be 2004) and the town becomes a stadium of hysterical devotees. The same thing happens, to a lesser extent, at the annual celebration on 3 December of the saint's death. Behind the casket, steps lead up to a small museum housing various portraits and relics attributed to Xavier, his life and times, as well as a collection of truly awful modern religious paintings, ham-fistedly executed after the style of Salvador Dali.

Across the road is the huge **Se Cathedral** (built 1562–1652). Dedicated to St Catherine of Alexandria, a pagan girl who embraced Christianity and was beheaded on the same date (25 November) that the Portuguese took Old Goa from the Muslims, it is one of Asia's largest churches, having 15 altars. The harmony of its façade was destroyed in 1776 when lightning demolished one of its twin bell towers. The remaining tower houses the famous 'Golden Bell' which would ring the death knell of burning heretics during the Inquisition and now sounds over a deserted city (*three times a day: 5.30am, 12.30pm, 6.30pm*) to be heard up to 6½ miles away. Walking up the crumbling staircase to view it is highly unsafe. The grand Renaissance cathedral is built in the Portuguese-Gothic style—its Corinthian interior is a Baroque riot of gilded carvings, with a vast barrel-vault ceiling and a glittering, gilded main altar (featuring painted scenes from the short life of St Catherine) which is the finest in India. Look at the 'miraculous' stone cross in one of the fourteen side-chapels. According to the guide, it 'grew' so high over the centuries that the ceiling had to be raised. Nowadays it's protected by a sturdy wooden support to stop relic hunters chipping away souvenirs. Undeterred, they chip away at the wood surround instead.

The nearby **Convent and Church of St Francis of Assisi**, notable for its two-storey façade crowned with twin octagonal towers, is one of Old Goa's most fascinating buildings. Originally a small Franciscan chapel (commenced in 1517), the present structure was constructed in 1661. It is notable for its richly carved woodwork, Renaissance frescoes and flooring of 16th-century gravestones, their heraldic devices announcing the deaths of well-born Portuguese. The **Archaeological Museum** to the rear (*open daily except Fri, 10–5*) has a poorly lit model Portuguese caravelle, while upstairs is an entertaining gallery of Portuguese ex-viceroys—possibly the worst portraits ever painted, each viceroy looking suitably corrupt and thuggish. More beautiful are the sculptures downstairs, recovered from the Hindu temples over which the great basilicas were built (great Christendom crushing the heathens etc. etc.).

Make sure you wander up to the tall ruin of the **St Augustine Tower**, where the nave of what was once a great church now lies open to the sky, under whose broken arches local tribeswomen gather and talk. After that head down to Old Goa's boat jetty, walking downhill towards it under the old Portuguese 'Gateway to India' arch. A ferry plies across the estuary to **Diwar Island**, from where a connecting bus takes you into the wonderful little demi-paradise of the island's interior—empty beaches, shady palm bowers, and rustic old Portuguese houses. A short, strenuous climb takes you up to the hilltop at the centre of the island, with memorable views from the church. Return down for a relaxing afternoon on the beach before getting the ferry back to Old Goa. Don't forget to bring a packed lunch.

If you decide to stay the night in Old Goa, you can find **accommodation** in the excellently named **Our Own Den Hotel** at Bella Vista, Corlim, ✆ (0832) 86194/86292, or at the **Hotel Juliet**, also in Corlim, ✆ (0832) 86311/2. Both are in the 'cheap' price range. Take an auto-rickshaw from the bus stand to Corlim for about Rs7–10.

Flea market, Anjuna

North Goa

North Goa's Beaches

I am writing this sitting in the doorway of our hut, with a glass of feni (the local spirit, distilled from cashew nuts) beside me, and through a fringe of palms, stirring in the evening breeze, I can see a fleet of ancient fishing boats sailing away into the gold and crimson sunset. But this is a place and a time for purple prose, so I must exercise restraint.

Dervla Murphy in Goa, *On a Shoestring to Coorg*

Fort Aguada

This jet-set resort, notable for its 16th-century fort (*open Mon–Fri, 4–5.30 only*) and apparently endless expanse of white sand, has the best water sports, the best coastal views and the most famous beach hotel in India. This is the Taj group's **Fort Aguada Beach Resort**, © (0832) 276201/276210. Rooms here start at US$60 single in the off season (July, August and September) rising to US$145 during the Christmas and New Year period. The best ones, with excellent views from large terraces, are in the main block. There are good facilities for water-skiing, windsurfing, parasailing, fishing and scuba-diving. Right next door is the equally fine **Taj Holiday**

Village, ✆ (0832) 27515, which offers charming beach cottages designed like Goan homes in a private, romantic setting. Prices start at US$45 in the low season for a non air-conditioned room in a cottage and reach US$130 in the high season for air-conditioned rooms. Single-bedroom cottages, two-room villas and family units are also available. The high level of service, the excellent facilities and special areas for children make the Holiday Village one of Goa's best options.

The state's most exclusive and ridiculously overpriced resort is at Aguada. The Taj's 20-villa **Aguada Hermitage**, ✆ (0832) 276201/276210, was built for the Commonwealth Heads of Government conference in 1982 and is situated on the hillside above the beach resort overlooking the sea. There are four types of villa with rates ranging from US$135 in the low season to US$475 during the Christmas–New Year period.

Candolim

Candolim is a beach that most independent travellers avoid. It has the long palm-fringed sands but is known for wind and lacks the social life of the northern beaches. It also gets crowded with Indian tourists at weekends.

There is a variety of accommodation here, however.

Candolim ✆ (0832–) ***Where to Stay***

luxury

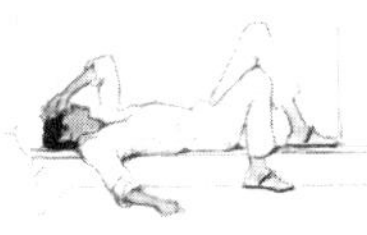

The **Taj Holiday Village** in Candolim, ✆ 27047/7733, is a large, self-contained resort with a stretch of private beach and watersport facilities. Very comfortable but a little bland. In the same price range is the **Whispering Palm Resort** on Waddi Candolim Beach, ✆ 886140/1/2. Here rooms can be bargained down to about Rs500 in the off season.

expensive

The **Holiday Beach Resort**, ✆ 276233/276088, has little character but is small, with just 20 rooms, and again you can negotiate much lower prices out of season. You can also arrange water sports and local day trips through the resort.

moderate

Right on the beach is the **Palm Spring Beach Resort** but this is often full. If so, the following all offer decent rooms near the beach: the **Alexandra Tourist Centre** on Murad Vaddo, ✆ 276097/276250, @ 276250; the **Marbella Guest House**, 77 Sinquerim (no phone); the **Altrude Villa** on Murad Vaddo, (no phone); and the **Sea Shell Inn**, ✆ 276131.

inexpensive

There a several reasonable places within this category but unfortunately none of them have telephones as yet. You have to turn up on the doorstep and negotiate for a room. However, they are all fairly close together so you can walk or take an auto-rickshaw between them without difficulty. Try the **Ave Maria Guest House**, the **Coqueirial Holiday Home**, or the B&B run by **Innocencia de Souza**. All are on Camtomim Vaddo.

cheap

Again, there are no telephone numbers for places to stay in this category. Try the **Pinto Beach Cottages** on the beach, house no. 81–9, the brilliantly named **Pretty Petal Guest House** at 824 Camtomim Vaddo or the **Manuel Guest House** on the same street. A number of families rent rooms: Isabel Fernandes, who lives at 73a Candolim Beach; Josephin Fernandes at 74–9 Escrivao Vaddo; Jacinta Cardoz, 71B/9 Escrivao Vaddo; Deodita Rodrigues, 1067 Escrivao Vaddo and Milagrina de Souza, Velina Villa, 23/A/10 Simer. If these particular people cannot accommodate you they will know someone who can.

Eating Out

New restaurants and beach shacks open (and close again) every season in Candolim. However, the village has two Old Faithfuls that have survived to become Goan institutions. The first of these is **21 Coconuts**, a Swiss-run, smartish beach shack at the beach end of the road that runs from Candolim's main street to the sea. It manages to produce a kind of European nouvelle cuisine (though with more generous portions) and is open for breakfast, lunch and dinner from October to March. Back on the main road is the much cheaper **Bob's Inn**, which serves great seafood, especially crab.

Calangute

The old 'Queen Beach' of Goa, where coconut palms once shaded a mile-wide stretch of tranquil orange sands, has sadly been overdeveloped and ruined by unsightly tourist hostels, souvenir stands and noisy, busy traffic. Bus loads of Indian voyeurs turn up here daily hoping to photograph Western women unclad on the beaches. Calangute is now a fully fledged Indian holiday resort with popcorn stands, iced beer stalls and shifty businessmen and is both dirty and commercial. Most travellers head straight on to Baga or Vagator but a few hang around for the 'action'. This includes a trio of useful travel agencies offering cheap international flights near the tourist office and various stalls selling cheap-and-nasty Indian crafts and good but pricey Tibetan/Rajasthani items. There are also some good eating places like **Souza Lobo Restaurant** (lovely beach setting, superb seafood and Indian wine), **Wilson's** (on the beach), **Alex Cold Drink House** (by the statue, with good sounds), **Modern Tavern** (cheap drinks) and **Dinky Bar & Restaurant** (nice Goan food). For travellers, Calangute's main function these days is as a shopping/communications/bank centre for those staying up in Baga, Vagator, Anjuna and the northernmost beaches. There are several STD/ISD places on Calangute's main road as well as a branch of the Wall Street Finance Company, where you can change travellers' cheques.

If you are intending to go from Calangute to Mapusa, try and stop along the way at **Saligao**, just 2 miles east of Calangute, where stands Goa's only neo-Gothic church, the **Church of the Rosary**, built in the 1870s. The building is a bit of a horror, like a stuccoed elephant carcass with spikes, but its architectural rarity warrants a visit. Saligao also has a great restaurant, **Florentine's**, and a Cottage Industries Emporium (the two are next door to each other). After shopping for handicrafts sit outside and eat the excellent (and cheap) chicken cafrael that is Florentine's speciality. Cooked with green spices and black pepper, it'll wake you up.

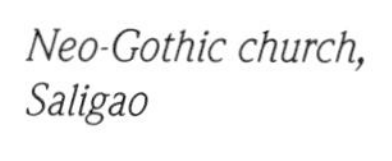

Neo-Gothic church, Saligao

Calangute ✆ (0832–)

Where to Stay

If you get stuck in Calangute en route for Baga and the northern beaches, here are some pointers.

expensive

The most expensive place in Calangute is the **Hotel Goan Heritage** on Gaura Vaddo, ✆ 276120/253/254/027, ℻ 276120. A large complex built around an old Portuguese house it offers good food but little atmosphere.

moderate

The best place to stay in Calangute is the charming **Varma's Beach Resort**, ✆ 276077, behind the bus stand with lovely gardens and homely air-conditioned rooms with verandahs. The **Concha Beach Resort**, ✆ 276056/078, at Umta Vaddo (on the beach) has a good restaurant, decent rooms and all services.

inexpensive

Towards the bottom end of this price range the clean, comfortable **Tourist Hostel**, ✆ 276024, is good value but often full and noisy. If it is full try to get in at either the **Hotel Mira** on Umta Vaddo (no phone) or the **Golden Eye** on Gaura Vaddo, which has clean, basic cottages.

cheap

If the various cheapies (mostly unsatisfactory) that you will undoubtedly hear about on the travellers' grapevine don't appeal, stay in a family house behind the beach. Here are some names to try: Annie Fernandes, 15 Gaura Vaddo; Agostino de Souza, E6/1 Cobra Vaddo; Antonio De Souza, 5/226 Umta Vaddo; Anthony de Souza, 189 Umta Vaddo; Cecilia Lobo, 1985 Cobra Vaddo or Bethe Andrade, 2231 Saunta Vaddo. Families often meet travellers off the bus and offer clean, simple, double rooms. These are recommended but have your mosquito net handy.

Baga

As you head north, the beaches become better and better. Baga, overlooked by a high promontory, is a fine example. Just 1½ miles north of touristy Calangute, it is far more secluded and pleasant, at least at its northern end near the forested headland that separates Baga from Anjuna Beach. A small river meets the sea at the base of this headland.

For relative quiet plus good facilities (it even has a small windsurfing school), Baga is still the best of Goa's northern beaches. If you want peace and quiet, stay in the wooded end north of the river from where you can reach all the beach-shack bars and restaurants but go home to a quiet haven under the coconut palms. To get a motorcycle over the river, cross via the concrete bridge, a mile's detour to the east.

Getting There

by bus

Only one service, at 5pm, goes from Panjim all the way to Baga. However, regular half-hourly services run from Panjim to Calangute, from where you can either walk along the pleasant beach or busy road or hire a motorbike taxi to take you and your gear the rest of the way.

by motorbike and bicycle

If staying in Baga it's a good idea to hire a motorbike, scooter or bicycle for trips to Panjim. Ride as far as Calangute then take the bus—the police run a racket of waving down Westerners on motorcycles near Panjim and demanding on-the-spot 'fines'.

Baga ✆ (0832–)

Where to Stay

moderate

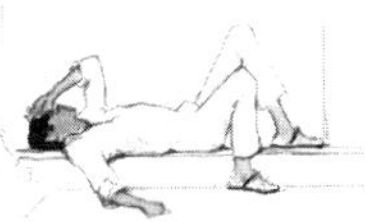

The **Hotel Baia Do Sol**, ✆ 276084, offers superb recreation (river cruises, water-skiing, yachting and fishing), good entertainment (traditional folk dances and music), great food (at the renowned **Seafood Restaurant**) and lovely riverside cottages on the seafront.

inexpensive

The **Riverside Hotel**, ✆ 276062, at the north end of Baga near the turn-off for the concrete bridge has a superb riverside location, a charming lady owner, delicious home cooking and roomy two-person cottages. Failing this try the **Sunshine Beach Resort** (no phone), a self-contained place with a pool built around its own courtyard behind the beach on the Baga–Calangute road.

cheap

Nani's and Rani's is a guest house on the north side of the river, owned by a friendly Indo-Portuguese family. They rent out small self-contained chalets set in a garden around their own old Portuguese villa, from which they run a very good restaurant and STD/ISD service.

If you cannot find a place at Nani's and Rani's, walk on 50 yards past their villa, then take the footpath's right-hand fork up through a grove palm trees. A number of small farmsteads are scattered on the wooded hill at the end of the palm grove and most have rooms for rent for very little. Often they can rent you a scooter or motorcycle as well and will provide morning tea, do the laundry and arrange taxis to and from the airport for an extra charge. Just walk up to the first house and ask and you will soon be directed to someone who has a room free.

The **Casa Portuguesa** at the Baga end of the Baga–Calangute road is the most expensive place in town but also one of the best in Goa for traditional local cuisine. You can eat on the verandah or in one of the spacious colonial dining rooms and even get the owner to sing some bad but passionate *fada* for you on his guitar. The restaurant occupies his grandmother's house and is about as traditional a place as you are likely to find on the tourist trail.

Many travellers also rate the **Riverside Restaurant** situated at the far northern end of Baga, right by the river. The prices are high but the prawn *balchao* is worth the extra rupees.

To be avoided for food is **Tito's**, Baga's most popular bar—a big American-style bar/restaurant full of package tourists and Indian boys from Bombay loudly on holiday. Everything at Tito's is grossly overpriced but it serves as a good orientation point as it sits at the top of a narrow road connecting the south end of Baga beach with the main Calangute road. It is also a good place to find out where the next all-night techno party is happening.

Much cheaper is the **Ancona**, a small Tibetan restaurant on the road between Tito's and the Calangute road. Run by a group of cousins, Ancona serves great *momos* (veg and meat), cornbread and hearty soups, as well as superb cakes. Two standard cheapies popular with backpackers are **Vicky's**, a seafood place/bar on the beach about halfway between Tito's and the river, and **Britos** at the north end of the Calangute road, which serves good Indian food (try the *sag paneer*) as well as slightly overpriced Western dishes.

For excellent value on the north side of the river, try **Nani's and Rani's**. The breakfasts here are particularly good; sit out on their verandah and eat stuffed pancakes and drink fresh juices. A little further along the headland footpath is the **Sunset Restaurant**, which does good, standard seafood under a palm-thatch awning that looks out over the Arabian sea.

Anjuna

Just 10 minutes' walk further north (cross the river at the top of Baga, walk round the headland past the chapel) is the 'freak beach' of Anjuna. A marvellous place for meeting people, illegal nude bathing or just hanging out, it has big pros and cons. It's famous for its beach parties, where everyone flips out on heavy techno

music and goes skinny-dipping. Also for its superb **Flea Market**, which takes place at the southern end of the beach every Wednesday between 2 and 7pm. This is a great place to sell your unwanted jeans, watch, camera or Walkman or shop around for Tibetan/Kashmiri jewellery, Rajasthani handicrafts, stylish cotton clothing and funky hippie handicrafts. The atmosphere is great. The whole of Goa seems to turn up, also loads of Arabs, Chinese and Indians, either to buy Western luxury items or just to 'see the hippies'. Anjuna itself is a small, attractive cove, backing onto swaying palms. The sea is very suitable for swimming, except in the afternoon, when it is swept by strong onshore breezes. At this time of day walk round to the quiet, protected coves between Anjuna and Baga which are beautifully secluded. In the town is the splendid 1920s **Albuquerque Mansion** (*open weekdays, 10–5*), a massive Portuguese villa, still partly inhabited, which operates as a kind of living museum.

Note: between November and February when all accommodation is booked weeks ahead, don't turn up on spec unless you're prepared to sleep on the beach for a few days.

Also, beware of smoking marijuana openly: police informers often spy out smokers, then plant large amounts of drugs in their bags, in advance of an out-of-the-blue 'official search' after which you will be 'fined' as much as the policeman in charge thinks you can pay.

Getting There

The most common approach to Anjuna is via local bus or shared cab from Mapusa (Rs7–10). But some travellers hire motorcycles from Calangute and bike up. These can be hired at Anjuna too for about Rs1000 per fortnight and are a popular, if injury-fraught, method of beach-hopping.

Sports and Activities

Healthier than raving is **parascending**. There is a school which operates on the cliffs above Anjuna throughout the Christmas season (as well as up at Arambol). To sign up for a course ask at the **Shore Bar**.

Anjuna © (0832–)

Where to Stay

inexpensive

There are just two proper lodges: **Bougainvillaea**, with overpriced, basic rooms but a lovely garden and good food; and the **Tamarind Lodge**, a collection of stone cottages (some with air-conditioning) on Kumar Vaddo about 2 miles from Anjuna beach and a well-known seafood restaurant. It's only worth staying here if you have your own transport.

cheap

The choice of lodges is very limited: try the **Poonam Guest House** near the flea market (though rooms here will be over Rs100 during the season), or **Grandpa's Inn**, © 26250, out on the Mapusa Road. Otherwise you have to find a room with a local family. If you intend to stay a long time you can negotiate very cheap rooms back off the beach. Ask at the **Shore Bar** at the south end of the beach and the owners there will put you in touch with someone.

Eating Out

Anjuna has some very good eating places: try **Tamarind Lodge** on Kumar Vaddo, about 2 miles from the beach, for traditional Goan dishes. Cheaper is **Poonam's** or the **Rose Garden Restaurant** on the beach. In the town is **O'Coqueiro**, © 267271, at Porvorim with excellent Goan food. For tasty snacks try the **German Bakery** near the flea market which serves good lasagne and tofu-oriented veggie food as well as breads and biscuits. **Grandpa's Inn** on the Mapusa Road offers an elegant setting in an old Portuguese villa. The German owners serve up a delicious mix of Goan and Western cooking accompanied by that rare treat in India—a green salad. And they are safe to eat too, being washed in filtered water before serving. Prices though are not cheap. If you want to make a night of it, ride your bike or take a motorbike taxi 4 miles towards Mapusa to **The Haystack** where you can hear live music and eat traditional Goan food and drink cheap, cheap local wine. Wherever you eat be aware that service at all Anjuna's restaurants is notoriously slow.

Entertainment and Nightlife

Most young travellers come to Goa for the **all-night techno parties**. These are grand affairs; outdoor raves, often right by the sea, held among luxuriant sub-tropical vegetation. Almost all the parties are held around Anjuna, Vagator and Arambol. The exact location tends to be kept secret until a few hours before but all the motorbike taxi men get tipped off on the day. The **Shore Bar** on Anjuna beach or the **Primrose** on the road to Vagator also good for finding out where parties are.

If you turn up around midnight when the local Indian men in search of a female tourist have got drunk and gone home, the parties can be magical, with local tribeswomen turning out with *chai* and cakes for sale, spreading mats on the ground for you to sit on and makeshift bars with beers illegally for sale. The parties are famed for having any amount of marijuana, acid and ecstasy.

A word of warning though, if you intend to 'trip', try not to wander too far afield, as the coastal country is incised with small ravines that are very easy to fall into. The local doctors make a good living from patching up people who have hurt themselves at parties, taken the wrong drug or crashed their motorbike. If you need **medical attention** at one of these parties, get a motorbike taxi immediately to **Dr Henriques Jawarharlal** whose clinic is on **Rodrigues Vaddo**, Siolim, near Vagator.

Chapora/Vagator

A 7-mile bus ride from Mapusa, these beaches are beautifully secluded. If you tire of Anjuna they are just a 1¾-mile stroll up along the headland. Vagator is strikingly beautiful, a small cove of rich orange sands embraced by green-gold coconut palms. (But avoid the picturesque rocky promontory at the centre of the beach: the locals use it as an outdoor loo.) The small sandy coves of Chapora adjoining it to the north are overlooked by the old **Portuguese Fort** (built 1717, now in ruins but worth a visit for the fine views from the ramparts), and back onto a charming little village.

Vagator ✆ *(0832–)*

Where to Stay

moderate

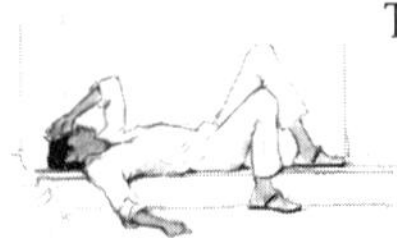

The upmarket place to stay is **Vagator Beach Resort**, ✆ 263276, with friendly atmosphere, good restaurant and lovely red-tiled beach-view cottages in the garden.

inexpensive

The **Royal Resort**, ✆ 263260, near the Vagator Resort, has some air-conditioned rooms, a decent restaurant and its own pool.

cheap

Dr Lobo's or **Noble Nest** are friendly and clean but basic. Otherwise here are some places to try for family rooms: Acacia Fernandes, 562 (1) Vagator; Agosthino Tinoco, 564 Vagator; the Anita Lodge, 511 Vagator; Apolin Fernandes, 526 Vagator; Carmina Morais, 581 Vagator; or Benvilla, 594 Vagator. If none of these have room they will soon put you in touch with somebody who does.

Eating Out

Eat at the big **Vagator Beach Resort** hotel, at **Lobo's** on the beach (not at the lodge of the same name in the village) or at the **Laxmi** on the beach. The **Primrose**, on the road between Vagator and Anjuna, serves cakes and desserts as well as the usual fish and chips-style beach food and is a good place to find out where the parties are being held (sometimes they are held right there).

Arambol/Terekol

These two northernmost beaches are the final retreat of the hippies and the place to really get away from it all. Bring a sleeping bag just in case you have to sleep on the beach but be careful not to let your belongings out of sight. Arambol has a beautiful freshwater lake (a little muddy, but pure and ideal for washing-off after swims in the salty sea), lovely sands, free camping, also beach huts and great expanses of empty beach. The friendly village close to the main beach has restaurants with reasonable food.

There are plans to build a huge 5-star hotel complex complete with golf course at

Arambol. The locals all oppose it, as they rely on the budget travellers for a living, and would make no money from rich tourists staying behind a high wall in the hotel compound. They also fear that their wells will be made dry by the golf course's tapping of the water table. However, until the hotel is actually built Arambol remains a paradise. A final ferry ride north of Arambol, **Terekol** beach marks the northern boundary of Goa's coast and has a fine Maratha fort, captured by the Portuguese in 1776 with a small church and good views.

Getting There

Arambol is 3 hours by **bus** from Mapusa or 4 hours from Panjim: a long trip, involving a **ferry** crossing at Siolim and then leaving the bus and taking a **shared taxi**, but well worth it. Terekol involves another ferry crossing at Keri, from which you need to take another shared taxi on to the fort. To call Arambol, phone the operator and ask for Redi followed by the number (manual exchange).

Where to Stay

cheap

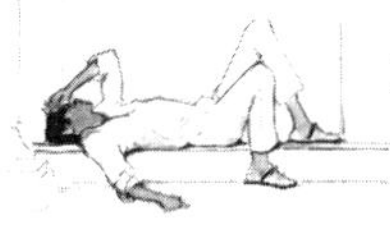

Try **Lizzy's Guest House**, Shri Benedict Fernandes house number 686, Arambol, or the **Hotel Miramar**, in Pednem, near the beach, for cheap, cleanish rooms. Otherwise it's rented rooms in family houses again. Walk from the beach to the small village of Waddo and ask for any of the following: Alex Fernandes, 660 (B) Khalcha Vadda, Bella Fernandes, 676 Socoilo Vaddo; Maria Rodrigues on Socoilo Vaddo, Paul de Souza, 665 Socoilo Vaddo; Sulochana Naik, 701 Khalcha Vaddo; Shreepad Mayekar, 688-A Arambol; or Uttam Kochrekar, at the Yellow House, 685 Khalcha Vaddo.

Terekol is the place to get away from things and you can stay at the fort, which has now been converted to the **Terekol Fort Tourist Rest Home**, book via Panjim or Margao tourist offices. Priced at between Rs100–350 per room per night, the fort offers accommodation in separate cottages. Otherwise, you have to stay in Arambol and walk up.

Vasco da Gama

Goa's least attractive town occupies a coastal promontory that juts out of the Marmagoa *taluka* into the Arabian sea roughly midway along the Goan coast. An industrial place, Vasco da Gama or 'Vasco' for short, has such delights as a petrol refinery (where fleets of tankers can load more than 1000 tons of crude oil per *hour*), an open-cast iron-ore mine (the ore crushed from the cliff directly above the harbour) and a small naval port. It is also the nearest large town to Goa's airport, 4 miles away at Diabolim; and Goa's central railway terminus, with connections to Bombay, Bangalore and Hospet via the broad-gauge link at Caranzol in the far east of Goa, near the Bhagwan Mahavir Wildlife Sanctuary.

In short, Vasco is a purely commercial centre and not a place to linger when on holiday. There are beautiful beaches nearby including **Bogmalo** (5 miles), with its exclusive and expensive Oberoi resort. Nearest to town (2½ miles) is **Hansa Beach** which has safe swimming but is marred by Vasco's industrial skyline. Just south of town (about half-a-mile from the railway station) is the infamous **Baina Beach**, by evening Goa's premier red-light district, with a tragically high incidence of HIV and AIDS.

Getting There

by air

Diabolim Airport, © 2788, is only two miles south of town. Both international and domestic flights come in daily. For full flight details, *see* **Travel**, p.9.

by train

The railway station is Swantantra Path. There are three daily services for the **Dudhsagar Falls** (3 hours) in the far east of the state, stopping at Margao and finally ending up at Caranzol in the Bhagwan Mahavir Wildlife Sanctuary (5 hours).

For rail links to **Bombay** and **Bangalore**, trains travel slowly to Miraj (about 5 hours) where there is a change to a broad-gauge line and another 20 hours to Bombay or Bangalore. Although the trip is leisurely and goes through some beautiful scenery, it is far quicker to take a bus for inter-state travel.

by bus

Bus services to Panjim and Margao leave from the bus stand on Swantantra Path every 30 minutes. There are also inter-state services (several daily) from Vasco da Gama running north to Bombay, south to Mangalore and Kerala and southeast to Bangalore. However, as these inter-state services also leave from the much more pleasant towns of Panjim and Margao, you are better advised to make long-distance trips from there.

by boat

Ferry services run from Marmagao Point, on the promontory west of town (at the foot of the ruined fort), to Dona Paula to the south across the Zuari Estuary. Services leave roughly once an hour between 9am and 6pm from September to May.

Tourist Information

The **Tourist Office,** ✆ (0834) 512673, is on the ground floor of the state-run **Tourist Hostel** on Swantantra Path by the bus stand.

The **State Bank of India** is at the northern end of F.L. Gomes Road, one block before the turning for St Andrew's church.

For **shopping** there is a **Government of India Emporium** at the Tourist Hostel on Swantantra Path near the bus stand.

The **post office** is one block east of the beach and one block up from the petrol refinery.

History

Vasco has always been Goa's principal port; its long narrow promontory dominates the natural harbour (one of the few on the whole Malabar Coast) as well as the entrance to the mighty Zuari estuary, Goa's largest. Unfortunately its old fort of Marmagao has been almost completely ruined over the centuries but in its day it was one of the strongest in the colony. During the Maratha invasion of 1683 it was this fort that housed the civilians of Old Goa and kept the colony's trade routes open. Despite various attempts to storm it the fort held until the Marathas were forced to abandon their conquest of Goa by the arrival of a Mughal army from Delhi. In the early 1700s there was a short-lived movement to relocate the capital here, but the colony's bureaucracy had become so unwieldly that the project was never realized and the filthy disease-ridden capital remained at Old Goa until its final move to Panjim in the mid 19th century. Marmagoa was allowed to fall into disrepair and the site of Vasco da Gama was only developed in the 20th century when it became clear that the colony needed a modern port. Consequently Vasco has a raw look and lacks the handsome Mediterranean charm of Goa's other large towns.

If you have to go to Vasco to catch a train, the **railway station** is at the eastern end of the central Dr Rajendra Avenue, where it meets the north–south road of Swantantra Path. Off this road, just southwest of the train station are the smelly vegetable and fish markets. At the far western end of Dr Rajendra Avenue is the dirty town beach fronting Marmagao Bay.

Where to Stay

Unlike Panjim and Margao, Vasco is not a place to find cosy inns. Unlike other places in Goa, the town can be very humid and most lodges have a problem with mosquitoes. However, prices are relatively cheap; shelling out a few extra rupees for air-conditioning is within most peoples' budgets.

moderate

If you have to spend a night here, you might try the **La Paz Gardens Hotel**, © 512121, a modern place with some air-conditioned rooms on Swantantra Path, about 200 yards north of the train station. Failing this, head for the **Rukmini Lodge**, © 512356, which is also on Swantantra Path but 150 yards south of the railway station. With a few air-conditioned rooms and decent Goan or south Indian food, this place is good value.

inexpensive

The state-run **Tourist Hostel**, © 513119, near the bus stand is also on Swantantra Path but about 100 yards north of the railway station. The hostel has good clean rooms, a few with air-conditioning, and a tourist office on the ground floor. Close to the fish market is the **Westend Lodge** on Flores Gomes Road. If the wind is blowing the wrong way this can make for a bit of a pungent stay, but again, some rooms are air-conditioned and there is a useful travel desk. Smaller and also central with some air-conditioned rooms is the **Gladstone Hotel** (no phone listed) on the Vila Ana, just off Dr Rajendra Avenue. A little out of the town centre is the quiet, family-run **Hotel Gangotri** on Casa Pravaca, © 512417.

cheap

The **Hotel Annapurna**, © 513517 on Dr Deshpande Road (parallel to and east of Swantantra Path) has a good reputation for clean, basic rooms as does the **Rebelo**, © 512620, just north of the sweaty town centre in the suburb of Mundvel.

Eating Out

There is little choice in Vasco but most places serve good Goan staples such as fried prawns, prawn and fish curries, *chourisso* and spicy chicken. Try the restaurant in the **La Paz Gardens** on Swantantra Path north of the train station, where you can sit outside under trees. If you don't like Goan food you can order vegetarian *thalis* and some Western dishes.

Just behind the beach near the Post Office is the **Flare Up**, which is more of a fast-food place but which serves good grilled fish and which gets the sea-breeze; bring your own booze. If you want a place with a bar try the **Little Chef** on the corner of Flores Gomes Road and Dr Rajendra Avenue. Again, you can choose between a Goan or a south Indian vegetarian menu.

North Goa Inland

I am brought back from a doze by the buzzing of bees probing holes in the bike's saddle for nesting sites. Propped up between the gnarled roots of a veteran mango tree, I let the soft breeze soothe away last night's Goan rum hangover.

Robin Brown, *Deccan Tamasha*

Mapusa

Mapusa sits at the crossroads of northern Goa and is the state's main market centre, serving both inland farmers and the villagers of the coast. You should visit for its **Friday market**, when people from all over Bardez pour in to do their weekly shopping. More Goan and less hippyish than the Anjuna flea market, the Mapusa market sells anything from glass bangles to water buffalo, is open from around 8am to 6pm, and is the cheapest place to shop in Goa. After the market, hang around for live music, folk dances and buffet at the **Haystack** (Friday nights from 8.30pm to very late).

Unusually for Goa there is little of architectural interest in Mapusa, which has grown up largely over the past twenty years. However, there is a beautiful church (there always is in Goa), **Our Lady of Miracles**, which dates from the late 16th century but was twice destroyed by fire. The present building went up after the last fire in the 1830s; it lies to the east of the town centre. Apart from the market, central Mapusa's only pretty feature is the large **Municipal Gardens**, on the east side of which you can pick up taxis and motorbike taxis.

Getting There

by bus

Buses run every half-hour to Panjim, Anjuna and Calangute. The bus stand is at the crossroads of the Anjuna and Market roads.

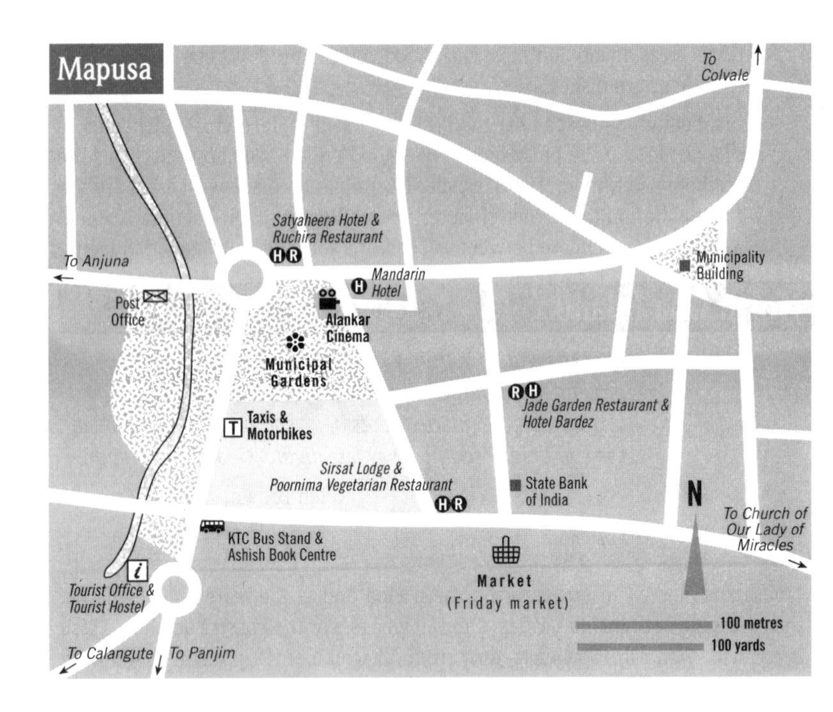

by taxi and motorbike taxi

These can be economical if shared: for example, a shared taxi to Panjim should not cost more than Rs10 per person but you'll have to bargain. Similarly, a motorbike taxi to Anjuna should cost about Rs10, shared between two but again you'll have to stick to your guns.

Tourist Information

The Tourist Office is on the ground floor of the Tourist Hotel on the traffic circle south of the Municipal Gardens, © 262390.

Mapusa © (0832–)

Where to Stay

moderate

The **Hotel Vilena**, © 263115, stands opposite the Municipal building and has a choice of clean, air-conditioned or non-air-conditioned rooms, as well as a fairly good Goan restaurant.

inexpensive

Try the pleasant **Tourist Hotel**, ✆ 262694, which has clean rooms and a nice rooftop bar/restaurant. Downstairs there is a useful little tourist office, which isn't much good for hard information but is okay for booking tours or bus tickets. If the Tourist Hotel is full, a good fall-back is the **Hotel Satya Heera** near the bus stand, ✆ 262849/262949, which has a few air-conditioned rooms.

cheap

Popular with backpackers are the **Hotel Bardez** on Coscar Corner, ✆ 262607, and the **Mandarin** opposite the Alankar Cinema.

Eating Out

For Goan cuisine eat out either at the **Casa Bela**, opposite the Hotel Vilena or the **Sanbhaya** round the corner. Both have superb seafood and Goan curry. Chinese food can be had at the **Mandarin** opposite the Alankar cinema. At the **Haystack** you can find a good, cheap south Indian menu, with some Western items and live music and dance on Fridays after the market. For a similar atmosphere try the **Blue Palm Restaurant** on the Anjuna Road, southwest of the Tourist Hotel. Cheaper *thali* options include the **Hotel Mahalaxmi** on Anjuna Road and the **Sirsat** opposite the market entrance. On the road between Panjim and Mapusa (near the Zuan bridge) is the **Cajueiro** or **Cashew Tree Restaurant**, a cheap but good place with a thatched roof and a dining room filled with plants. Try the squid or lobster and take your own booze.

Mayem and Bicholim

The *taluka* of Bicholim sits to the north of Panjim and east of Mapusa, separated from Mapusa town by the Mapusa river. The region is mainly worth exploring for its unspoilt countryside, sleepy villages and general atmosphere of calm. However, there are one or two specific tourist sites. The principal of these is **Mayem Lake**, whose wooded shores are home to a variety of birdlife and which sits in a landscape of low hills. You can hire pedal boats to go out onto the water from the **Lake Resort**, ✆ (0832) 32144, which also offers inexpensive accommodation in self-contained cottages (some air-conditioned) and cheaper dormitory beds. Avoid the place at weekends though, as it gets overrun by Indian tourists who shatter the calm of the place. Mayem is easily reached from Panjim by bus (journey about one hour) with buses leaving every half-hour.

From Mayem the road continues north through the little regional town of Bicholim, to the village of **Sanquelim**. This is the place where the colonial government settled its Rajput mercenaries (known as the 'Ranes') in the mid-1700s and where the same mercenaries staged their successful uprisings during the 19th century (*see* p.41), sometimes keeping the more pusillanimous Portuguese troops occupied for up to three years at a time. Sanquelim has two modern and rather ugly Hindu temples. Of more interest are the **Arvalem Caves**, about a mile from Sanquelim (signposted from the south-eastern end of town). Dating from the 6th or 7th centuries, these caves were cut from the rock-face by Buddhist monks. Like the cave sanctuary at Rivona in southern Goa (*see* p.110), these caves only ever provided the most simple of dwellings—tiny sleeping cells clustered near a main chamber of worship. Again, like the Rivona caves, it seems that these ones at Arvalem were abandoned, perhaps during the rule of the fiercely Hindu Vijayanagars (check spelling), and the worship turned over to Shiva—as the lingam in the main cave suggests. A short 10-minute drive from the caves, **Arvalem Waterfalls** are worth visiting after the monsoon (in October) when they cascade noisily through the surrounding trees, but through the dry winter the flow is reduced to a trickle.

Sanquelim can be easily reached by bus from Mapusa (about 2 hours), but you will have to walk for about half an hour or take a motorbike taxi to get out to the caves or the falls.

Where to Stay

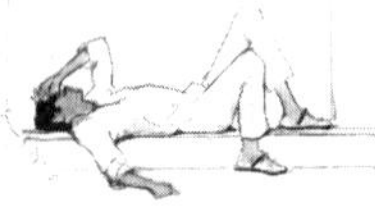

If you decide to spend the night in Bicholim *taluka*, Bicholim town has a very cheap but clean guest house called the **Hotel Sharada**, on Sander Path.

South Goa

South Goa's Beaches

This is being another slightly unreal day; it is just too idyllic to waken on golden sand in a palm-leaf hut, and to look through a non-door at a milky-blue early sky, and to hear the gentle hiss of the surf behind a shrieking of parrots and the immemorial chant of fishermen beaching their boats.

Dervla Murphy in Colva, *On a Shoestring to Coorg*

Dona Paula

About 5 miles south of Panjim via the village of Cavanzalem is the small, sandy cove of Dona Paula. An exclusive beach, it is pretty well dominated by one expensive resort hotel, the **Cidade de Goa**. However, even if you can't afford to stay here, Dona Paula is a worthwhile day trip from Panjim (there are buses every half-hour), and there are ferries (again, every half-hour) across to **Marmagao**, the northern industrial suburb of Vasco da Gama (*see* p.85). Along the Panjim–Dona Paula road, there are also two very good cheap restaurants.

Where to Stay

expensive

The **Cidade de Goa Beach Resort,** ✆ 221301/6/7, occupies the prime strip of beach near the jetty. The resort has well designed apartments, offers most watersports and has good food.

moderate

Not far from the Cidade de Goa is the **Villa Sol Hill** resort, ✆ 225045/225825, which offers slightly fewer luxurious apartments than its rival but also has watersports and good seafood at a fraction of the price.

inexpensive

Dona Paula's budget accommodation is set back about ¾-mile from the beach. Good, basic rooms can be had at the **Hotel Sea View,** ✆ 223327, and the **Mar Bravo,** ✆ 224348.

Eating Out

Try the inexpensive **Crosshill Bar** by the main roundabout in Dona Paula village. An unassuming place, it does fantastic fresh grilled fish. Turn left immediately after the Crosshill Bar, then left again and you come to the **White House**, another budget place that offers excellence way above its prices. Moreover, you can sit on the verandah and look out over the Mandovi River. Try the prawns or garlic mussels.

Bambolim and Goa Velha

Another sheltered beach cove, this time with no hotel, **Bambolim** is about 4 miles east of Dona Paula and is easily reached by bus or auto-rickshaw. The little beach itself makes a good place for a quiet swim before heading further east along the coast to the village of **Goa Velha**, just north of which is the **Pilar Seminary**.

Founded in 1613 by the Capuchin Monks (known for their intense devotion to the vow of poverty), the seminary has a beautiful old church whose plaster altar-piece depicting the Madonna was brought by the monks from their Church of Our Lady of Pilar in Spain. The seminary flourished until 1835 when all religious orders barring the Carmelite nuns were ejected from Goa. It was then looked after by the Carmelites but fell into increasing disrepair until its re-colonization in 1940 by the Missionary Society of St Francis Xavier. Their new seminary chapel is unusually fine for a modern church building, with an airy feel to its marble-pillared spaces.

The actual village of Goa Velha is thought to stand on the site of the ancient city of Gova, the Kadamba capital that was completely destroyed by the Bahmani Sultans in 1470 (*see* p.36).

The coast road continues south of Goa Velha for a few miles to the village of **Agassim**, from where a bridge leads across the Zuari estuary into Marmagao *taluka* and the main southern beaches. If you have time, stop in Agassim's early 17th-century church to drop your jaw over the huge, ornately gilded altarpiece, which testifies to wealth that even Goa's provincial churches enjoyed during the first 100 years of Portuguese rule.

Where to Stay

inexpensive

If you find yourself stuck for a night in Goa Velha, head for the **Mansao Serena**, an old Portuguese colonial villa near the market place. The rooms are basic but clean, and there is a lovely verandah. The owners will cook Goan-style seafood on request.

Bogmalo

This is one of Goa's best beaches, a secluded crescent-shaped cove with calm waters for swimming (a contrast to the powerful breakers of the more open beaches) and a friendly fishing village. Behind the beach rises the small upland of the Marmagao peninsula. But Bogmalo is an exclusive beach, presided over (as at Fort Aguada) by a single luxury hotel: the **Oberoi Bogmalo Beach**, ✆ (0834) 513291/311, ✉ (0834) 243303. If you can afford it, at only 5 minutes' drive from the Diabolim airport, this is an excellent holiday option with marvellous water sports, freshwater swimming pool, quality multi-cuisine restaurants, breezy open-air barbecues and elegantly furnished rooms, each one with a private balcony overlooking the sea. Few budget travellers make it out here: transport is too awkward (1 hour minimum by bus from Panjim, with a change at the 'Aerodrome' stop 2 miles before Vasco) and there's nowhere cheap to stay. Oberoi lays on free transport from the airport for residents.

South of Bogmalo are the Velsao and Majorda beaches. Both remain fairly quiet, and again there is a single luxury hotel, the **Majorda Beach Resort**, ✆ (0834) 220025/6 or 220164, ✉ 220212, set slightly back from the beach with all facilities.

Colva

Goa's longest beach is 12 unbroken miles of virgin white sand. Like Calangute to the north, Colva has been spoiled by progress—crowds of Indian men hassle Western women, there are inflated hotel and food prices, as well as aggressive hawkers. Now a money-making town receiving thousands of package tourists every year, Colva is no longer for the backpacker. However you need only walk a mile or two south of the main tourist drag to have the beach almost to yourself. The waters are warm and calm and the only people you'll see are local fishermen.

Getting There

Colva is a half-hour **bus** journey from Margao or a cheap **shared taxi** ride—pick one up from the taxi rank behind the Karmat Magdoot Restaurant on the right hand side of the Municipal Gardens in Margao.

Shopping

At the Colva bus stand there are a few pleasant shops, including **Damodar**, the place to buy or sell second-hand books. Reading is the main occupation on the beaches, so stock up. **Navneeta Handicrafts** is the place to buy cool, practical beach clothes. Other good purchases on the beach are beautiful lacquer boxes, eggs and painted shells. Buy cheap, attractive jewellery at Colva's Full Moon parties which some say are better than Anjuna's (they are certainly more mainstream) with an illuminated marquee: great music and dancing, and lots of atmosphere.

Colva ✆ (0834–)

Where to Stay

expensive

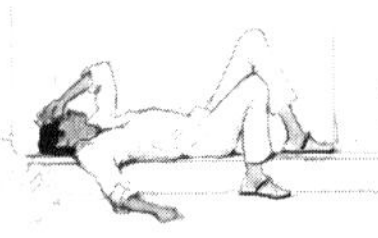

The **Penthouse Beach Resort**, ✆ 721975, has no penthouses, being laid out in separate cottages (some with air-conditioning) around a swimming pool and garden. Many travellers recommend this place for its relaxed atmosphere and friendly, helpful staff. Since renovation, prices of rooms at the air-conditioned **Hotel Silver Sands**, ✆ 721645, ℻ 737749, have soared to the top of this price category in the high season. Still, you get all the luxury facilities, including swimming pool, health club, windsurfing, travel office and free airport transfer.

moderate

There are several smaller resort hotels in this category, the **Colva Beach Resort,** ✆ 221975, the **Sukhsagar Resort**, ✆ 221888, the **William Beach Resort**, ✆ 221077, and the **Longuinhos Beach Resort**. Of the three, the Longuinhos is the favourite, being right by the beach, some rooms having balconies and a good restaurant. The others all have clean, comfortable rooms with a few air-conditioned (though you don't really need it so near the sea) and facilities for arranging watersports, day trips, etc.

inexpensive

The **Colmar**, ✆ 721253, is at the top end of this price range and offers either small cottages set in gardens or a cheaper dorm for backpackers. The restaurant is cheaper then the other resort hotels but is just as good. Try also the **Whitesands Hotel**, ✆ 721253. Right on the beach, it is good value with clean, non air-conditioned rooms and good food.

At the lower end of the range avoid the state-run **Tourist Hostel**, often full and much-frequented by Indian tourists and head for the **Sea View Cottages** opposite the Silver Sands Hotel instead. If full, try in some of the guest houses: **Glowin's Abode** and the **Vailankanni** are both on the street behind the beach (4th Ward) and are popular with travellers for their friendly owners and clean rooms. You might also try **Hotel Vincy**, ✆ 722276, above Vincy's Bar. This used to be very popular with independent travellers but has apparently fallen off a little lately, perhaps owing to the vast choice of more upmarket accommodation now available. A short bicycle ride from the beach are the **Garden Cottages** near the popular Johnny's Restaurant.

cheap

Many people are quite happy to put up at one of the many cheap lodges near the beach—after all, all you really need here is a bed for the night. A couple of goodies are **Fisherman's Cottage** (200 yards from the bus station with friendly people) and the nearby **Rose Cottages**. Also try **Maria's Guest House**, **Rodson's Cottages** or **Bruno's** on the 4th Ward or the **Tourist Nest**, 2 miles inland, which also has bicycles to hire.

During the high season when beach accommodation is very thin on the ground, try family houses like **Sabfran Tourist Cottages**, about two-thirds of a mile before Colva beach (ask the bus driver to drop you off) which charge less than Rs1500 per *month* for clean, habitable double rooms. Many of the houses on the 4th Ward rent cheap rooms and just wandering down the street with your backpack should be enough to bring out offers. Bargain down to just over half the asking price.

Eating Out

Most Colva residents eat at one of the ramshackle (but good) beach restaurants situated right on the shoreline. Regular favourites—all serving excellent seafood in addition to the usual pancakes, chips and omelettes—are **Sunset**, **Lucky Star** and **La Mir**. This is where people come to enjoy tasty fish dishes, spaghetti 'sizzlers' and a *feni* nightcap after a hard day's sunbathing. In the morning they pile over to **Umita Corner Restaurant and Bar** (away from the beach, near Tourist Nest) for breakfast. Recommended, and less than a mile from the beach, is **Sucorina**, which is good for seafood.

There's always a small gathering around the kiosks by the roundabout at 9 each morning when hot doughnuts arrive.

Benaulim

If mainstream Colva is too busy for you, stroll a mile down the sands to quiet, secluded Benaulim beach—far cheaper and more pleasant than Colva.

Benaulim has a pretty fishing village behind the beach, full of quaint, sleepy old Portuguese houses and buildings. The noise and 'tourist business' hustle of Colva fall away and you are back in quiet, rural Goa. There are a variety of places to stay and eat, both on the beach and in the village, but the village has the more sheltered accommodation—the beach can be shadeless and windswept. Hire a bicycle, which most lodges rent out for Rs20–30 per day, for getting to and from the beach.

Getting There

Direct **buses** run almost every half-hour from Margao, and a **shared taxi** can be picked up from behind the Karmat Magdoot restaurant on the east side of the Municipal Gardens in Margao. An **auto-rickshaw** costs between Rs30–45 depending on how much of hurry you are in and how good you are at bargaining. Journey time is approximately 30 minutes.

On the Beach

moderate

The **Carina Beach Resort** has very clean rooms, some with air-conditioning, and a good restaurant. However, it's more fun to eat at one of the beach shacks.

inexpensive

L'Amour Beach Resort, © 223720/6, is right on the beach, with nice clean rooms, some with a bath, but disappointing overpriced food. You can also try the **O'Palmar Beach Cottages,** © 223278, where the rooms have showers but whose hotel compound is a little windswept.

In Benaulim Village

cheap

Brito Tourist Corner at the village crossroads offers large rooms with balconies, as does **Rosarios's** on Vasvaddo, which also hires bikes and arranges transport to and from the airport. Vasvaddo has some other good cheapies like the **Palm Grove**, **More Cottages**, the **Bamboo Grove Cottages**, **Jack Joana Tourist Home**, **Fern Cottages**, the **Anita Tourist House**, **Amal Guest House** and the **Alfa Tourist Live-Inn**. All offer decent double rooms with attached bathrooms and Indian or European-style loos.

Eating Out

On the beach eat at the **Splash Restaurant**, which has good service and nice seafood, but steer clear of the pork sausages which, like sausages everywhere in Goa, come from pigs whose diet is principally one of human faeces. **Xavier's** has superlative fish dishes and reasonable sounds. **Pedro's** has gone into steep decline, but **Johncy's**, always packed and popular, though not always serving the best food, still has jolly beach parties.

Cavelossim, Varca and Mabor

These adjacent stetches of sand are really just extensions of Benaulim's long, lonely southward sweep of sand that heads down towards Betul.

There are a few over-priced isolated package-style hotels here, full of people looking a little bored and wondering where the famous zest of Goa can have disappeared to. However, in the off-season, these hotels can be bargained down to about a third of their asking price, and by staying in them you can guarantee some isolation.

For orientation, the beaches run like this: Varca in the north, Cavelossim in the middle and Mabor in the south. Varca village is a mile behind the beach, Cavelossim village is 2 miles inland from Cavelossim beach and Mabor village is right on the beach.

Getting There

Several **buses** run out to these villages from Margao each day but you have little chance of finding anyone to share a taxi with, as few travellers head here. An auto-rickshaw will cost near to Rs50. Journey time is approx 40 minutes.

Cavelossim, Varca, Mabor ✆ (0834–)

Where to Stay

luxury

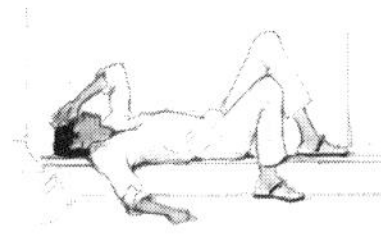

The **Goa Renaissance Resort** at Varca Village, ✆ 245200/245218, 📠 245225, offers the usual Goan style of luxury—air-conditioned rooms overlooking the sea, watersports, good food and a private stretch of beach to enjoy. The hotel, supposedly designed by Hawaiian architects, has a 6-hole golf course, a series of swimming pools and direct access to the beach.

Another 5-star property is **The Leela Beach** at Mabor, ✆ 246363/73, 📠 246352, with rooms in villas, 'pavilions' or private suites.

expensive

The **Holiday Inn Resort** at Mabor, ✆ 246304/5/6, 📠 246333, and the rather run-down **Old Anchor Resort**, ✆ 23005, with watersports facilities.

inexpensive

The **Graffino Beach Resort** between Cavelossim beach and village, ✆ 246315/9, is considerably cheaper than the other resorts, largely because it cannot offer air-conditioned rooms. A small place, it can make a nice out-of-season hideaway. It also has excellent food.

Eating Out

Whether you're staying in luxury or on a shoe-string, head for the cheap bar and grill called **Pinto's** in

Varca village, set on the corner of the main street and the signposted road to the Leela Resort. The restaurant's cheap prices (under Rs100 per head) does not mean the place is dingy—Pinto's has a great upstairs terrace for eating outside, and people came from all over the state to try its *chourisso* and seafood. Also in Varca village is **Natty's**, a newly opened Chinese restaurant that is also cheap and has (unusually for Goa) very efficient service.

Closer to the beach is the **Gato Loco**, ✆ (0834) 45050, 'Mad Cat', which serves excellent seafood and Indian cuisine—both northern and southern. If you go on a Wednesday, you get a three-course meal, a band and *fado* singers for Rs250 per head.

Betul

This lovely beach, located on the estuary of the river leading off from the bottom of Benaulim's 6-mile long swathe of sand, is serviced by direct buses from Margao. Almost untouched by tourism, Betul offers seclusion, magical beaches and unspoilt scenery. At present there is just one decent place to stay—a small lodge-cum-restaurant, run by a friendly Goan, right next door to an ancestral summer-house. This is a very well-run establishment with rooms with a balcony overlooking the river from Rs100. It is tricky to find. If coming in by bus you still have to walk across the river via the bridge. Another problem is lack of direct access from the lodge to the beaches. You either have a half-hour walk over the hills to a secluded, idyllic beach or you take a ferry across to the main beach, which runs down from Colva. Betul represents, for the time being at least, the perfect little getaway for the peace-loving beachcomber.

Cabo de Rama Fort

South of Betul, the main coast road turns inland for about 23 miles and the coast-line can only be reached by small dirt tracks accessible from the main road by motorbike or on foot. There *are* hidden caves and beaches to be found but you swim at your own risk—the author cannot vouch for the safety of the currents. There is also an old coastal fort, Cabo de Rama, taken by the Portuguese from the Vijayanagars. The site is named after the warrior Rama (one of Vishnu's avatars) who apparently lived on the headland during his period of exile. Today, the long-abandoned fort is only partly ruined and still has some of its big cannons. Be warned though—the road (signposted about 8 miles south of Betul) is rough and taxi drivers will demand high prices to venture down it.

Palolem

A little more developed than Betul, Palolem is still one of the cheapest and quietest of Goa's beach enclaves. Its small village is strung out under the palms and has two beaches. The main one, a 2-mile golden crescent complete with fishing boats and beach shack restaurants runs between two forested headlands. The smaller beach, south of the southern headland, can be yours all day with almost no disturbance.

Getting There

Palolem is the southernmost tourist spot in Goa, reached by a 2-mile sideroad from the town of Canacona. **Buses** run to Palolem from Margao every hour (as well as down the Karnataka coast to Gokarn and Mangalore), but to get out to Palolem you have to take either an **auto-rickshaw** (don't pay more than Rs25) or a **motorbike taxi** (about Rs10).

Palolem ✆ (0834–)

Where to Stay

inexpensive

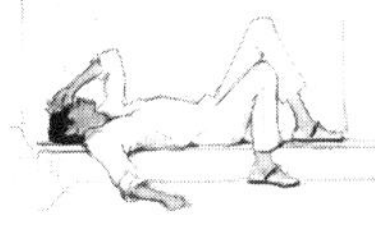

Palolem's one resort hotel, the imaginatively named **Palolem Resort** has self-contained chalet-style rooms with attached bathrooms or very comfortable cheaper safari tents with a shared ablution block, set in a small garden right on the beach. There is a smaller resort of palm-thatch huts next door but it is booked through the Indian Tourist Office in Bombay and is always full.

cheap

There are several places where you can rent family rooms two-thirds of a mile into the coconut groves, behind the beach. The best place to start looking is at **Jackson's**, a shabby bar/general store 50 yards south of the turn-off for the beach along the Canacona road. The owner can be a little brusque and charges inflated prices for his rooms but if you stick to about half what he asks (he asks about Rs80, you offer Rs40–50), he will show you to someone who can rent at that price.

Rajabag

The southernmost beach in Goa has no development at all. The only place to stay is a lonely hotel, often all-but empty, 1½ miles behind the beach, involving a walk through sand-scrub and cashew bushes. The hotel is reached from Canacona by auto-rickshaw or motorbike taxi (same prices as for Palolem), or from Palolem by walking 3 miles to the south and staying parallel with the coast where the road forks off to Canacona. A very pleasant walk in the morning or evening, Rajabag makes a good day trip from Palolem.

Rajabag ✆ (0834–)

Where to Stay

inexpensive

If you decide that you like the solitude of Rajabag, the **Molyma Hotel**, ✆ 643082, @ 643081, is a mile away, sitting south of the junction of the footpath to the beach and the road from Canacona. Unfortunately the building itself is rather bland and modern, but its pleasant little garden and tennis court make up for that and you cannot help feeling sad for the owners who cannot have recouped their investment. The food is quite good as long as you stick to Indian items and avoid the prawns, which are of the disappointing, small, packaged variety.

South Goa Inland

In the distance a huddled, red-roofed village squats between two humped hills, each crowned with a small fort.

Robin Brown, *Deccan Tamasha*

Margao

Handsome, colonial Margao is Goa's southern urban centre and a thriving commercial town. It has parks, modern buildings and a very Latin flavour. The residential streets radiating out from the central square that encloses the **Municipal Gardens** boast some of Goa's most beautiful old Portuguese mansions, with balconies, patios, terraces and red-tiled sloping roofs—still inhabited by descendents of the families who built them 200 years ago. This is the jumping-off point for Colva, Benaulim and Cavelossim beaches, as well as for exploring the inland towns of Chandor and Rachol with their great churches and villas. Most folk just pass through on their way to the beaches, but if you have more than a week in Goa it is worth spending an afternoon in Margao to visit one of its splendid villas and to try the food in one of its excellent tavernas.

Tourist Information

The **Tourist Office**, ✆ (0834) 222513, is on the ground floor of the **Tourist Hostel**, on Miranda Road just behind the Municipal Building that sits at the south end of the Municipal Gardens. One branch of the **State Bank of India** is on Miranda Road, east of the Tourist Hostel near the corner of Inacio Loyola Road, and another branch is on a street to the east of the Municipal Gardens. The main **post office** is at the northern end of the Municipal Gardens, opposite the small children's playground. For any travel arrangements, a very good **travel agent** is Paramount Travels, ✆ 221150, 732572, opposite the Tourist Office. Paramount staff are models of efficiency and are very good at getting you the cheapest deal, especially on domestic flights.

For **shopping**, there are bargains to be had at the main **market** off Station Road, just southeast of the Municipal Gardens.

Getting There

by train

There are several daily services between Margao and Vasco da Gama, as well as up to Dudhsagar Falls and Caranzol in the mountains. The train is slow, but the trip to the mountains (about 3 hours) makes a great change from the beaches. The railway station is on Station Road, which runs southeast from the Municipal Gardens (about half a mile).

Old colonial architecture, Margao

by bus

Margao has, rather irritatingly, three bus stands. The main **Kadamba** terminus is about a mile-and-a-half north of the Municipal Gardens via A Bade Faria Road. It's a fag getting out there from the town centre (a hot walk or an auto-rickshaw ride), but if you want to get a seat you are best advised to go there as the other two bus stands, on the **west side** of the Municipal Gardens (for buses north) and the **east side** (for buses south), are very crowded and chaotic and not the places to get on if you are loaded down with bags.

Local buses to **Panjim** and **Vasco da Gama** leave about every half-hour from Kadamba, as well as to the south and east, including Palolem, Ponda and most other Goan towns. You can also pick up buses to the beaches at Colva, Benaulim, Mabor, Cavelossim and Betul and these also leave about once every half-hour.

Several inter-state buses leave daily for **Bombay**, **Bangalore**, **Mangalore** and the Kerala coast from Kadamba Bus Station. Make your reservations at Paramount Travels opposite the Tourist Hostel and Tourist Office on Miranda Road (*see* above).

by taxi and auto-rickshaw to the beaches

Rather than wait for a bus to get out to the beaches, only 20–25 minutes by auto-rickshaw or shared taxi, which you can pick up anywhere around the Municipal Gardens. However, you won't get away with a ride for less than Rs30–40 (and this with hard bargaining) unless you take a **shared taxi**. These will cost you anything between Rs10 and 20 per person depending on how many of you there are (and again, it takes a bit of bargaining). You pick up the shared taxis from behind the Kamat Magdoot restaurant on the right-hand side of the Municipal Gardens.

The Town

The town of Margao has several sites worth a visit. Try to get to the **da Silva House** or House of the Seven Shoulders (*open by appointment, contact the Tourist Office at the Tourist Hostel, Miranda Road*) begun in the late 17th century and marked out by its three high roof gables and its handsome Indo-Baroque façade. Now run as as a museum (and reduced to only a third of its original size), this great villa is one of the grandest in Goa. There is an impressive staircase of polished rosewood (most of the house's beautiful furniture is carved from this wood), a solemn family chapel and a courtyard garden full of flowers. The house is still owned by a da Silva (the ninth generation to live there!). Visitors are asked to make a donation—about Rs200 for a small group.

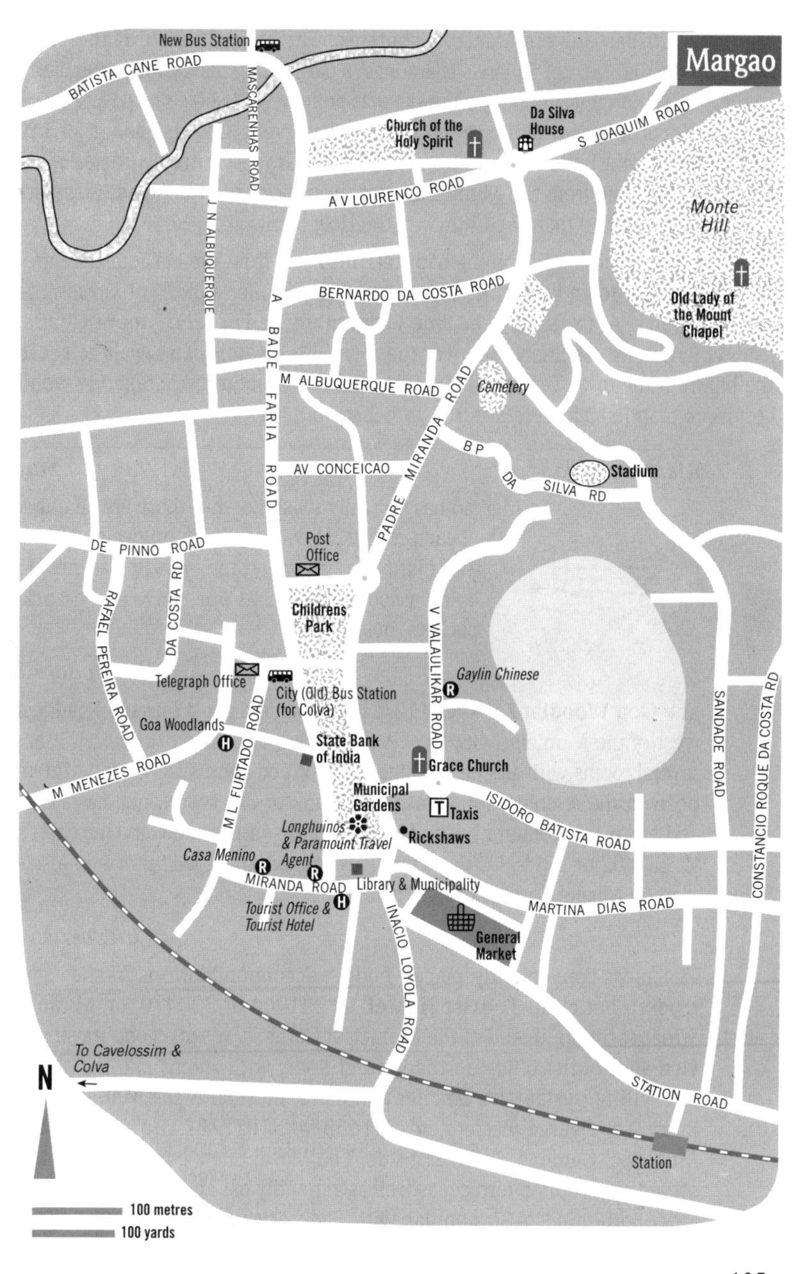
Margao
New Bus Station
BATISTA CANE ROAD
MASCARENHAS ROAD
Church of the Holy Spirit
Da Silva House
S JOAQUIM ROAD
A V LOURENCO ROAD
J N ALBUQUERQUE
Monte Hill
BERNARDO DA COSTA ROAD
Old Lady of the Mount Chapel
A BADE FARIA ROAD
M ALBUQUERQUE ROAD
Cemetery
PADRE MIRANDA ROAD
B P DA SILVA RD
Stadium
AV CONCEICAO
DE PINNO ROAD
Post Office
Childrens Park
RAFAEL PEREIRA ROAD
DA COSTA RD
V VALAULIKAR ROAD
Telegraph Office
City (Old) Bus Station (for Colva)
Gaylin Chinese
Goa Woodlands
M L FURTADO ROAD
State Bank of India
Grace Church
M MENEZES ROAD
Municipal Gardens
Taxis
ISIDORO BATISTA ROAD
SANDADE ROAD
CONSTANCIO ROQUE DA COSTA RD
Longhuinos & Paramount Travel Agent
Rickshaws
Casa Menino
MIRANDA ROAD
Library & Municipality
Tourist Office & Tourist Hotel
INACIO LOYOLA ROAD
MARTINA DIAS ROAD
General Market
To Cavelossim & Colva
N
STATION ROAD
Station
100 metres
100 yards

More grandly Baroque are Margao's churches. The huge **Church of the Holy Spirit** on the Old Market Square sits amongst a particularly handsome group of private villas. The original church on the site was built in the 1560s, sacked and burnt by the soldiers of Bijapur in the 1580s and then lay derelict and abandoned for 150 years. The present building dates from 1675. The **Grace Church**, situated more centrally just uphill from the Municipal Gardens on Isidor Batista Road, is smaller and less monumental than the Church of the Holy Spirit.

If the day is not too hot, climb the **Monte Hill**, rising from the residential quarter northeast of the town centre. Its tree-covered slopes offer a pleasant morning or evening ramble. At the top sits the little 17th-century **Lady of the Mount Chapel** from where there are fine views over the town. It's a complicated walk to get to the hill from the town centre, but an auto-rickshaw or motorcycle taxi ride won't cost more than Rs10 for a return trip *if* you bargain.

Margao ✆ (0834–)

Where to Stay

Margao has no really swish hotels—those are all out at the beach resorts. However, if you do decide to stay the night, there are some very pleasant old colonial lodges as well as one or two good backpackers' hostels.

moderate

The **Goa Woodlands**, ✆ 221121, is on Miguel Loyola Furtado Road just west of the Municipal Gardens. An old-fashioned, family-run hotel, it has several rooms with air-conditioning. If the Woodlands is full try the **Metropole** on the Avenida Conceicao, ✆ 221552 or 221169, which has a pool and a rooftop restaurant. The **Hotel La Flor** on Erasmo Carvalho Street, ✆ 221402 or 221591/7, also provides comfort and good service on a side road off Miguel Loyola Furtado Road.

inexpensive

The most conveniently placed budget accommodation is in the ugly, modern but clean **Tourist Hostel**, ✆ 221966 or 220470, on Miranda Street at the south end of the Municipal Gardens. It has a good travel service and tourist office on the ground floor, with rooms and a clean, if unexciting, restaurant. Smaller and more informal is the **Mabai** in the Praca Dr George Barreto, ✆ 221653/4/5/6/7/8, also just off the Municipal Gardens on the east side. The Mabai offers good Goan cuisine served on a rooftop terrace, as well as a friendly bar and some rooms with air-conditioning. Also popular with backpackers is the **Silveirado** on

Monte Hill, © 220407, which has the advantage of the hill breezes and views over the town.

cheap

Margao is not a comfortable place to stay in really cheap lodges—nights can be hot and humid and there are mosquitoes. If you are looking to stay somewhere in this category, you are much better advised to grab a bus or auto-rickshaw and head out to Benaulim, to one of the pleasant, cheap beach-side lodges such as Rosario's (*see* p.98). However, if you have to stay the night in Margao, the following lodges are not too bad: the **Rukrish** on Francisco Luis Gomes Road, near the railway station and opposite the Bank of India; the nearby **Greenview** on Station Road, © 220151; the **Sanrit**, opposite the railway station, © 221226/2/7; and the **Paulino**, © 220615, just east of the town centre in the suburb of Pajifond.

Eating Out

Margao has some of the state's best restaurants. The **Casa Menino** (expensive) and **Longhino's** (inexpensive), both opposite the Municipal building, are both excellent for Goan food. Try the spiced crabs, pickled fish or chicken cafrael. On V Valaukilar Road, parallel with the east side of the Municipal Gardens, is **Gaylin** (moderate), one of Goa's best Chinese restaurants. Order the stir-fried prawns with cashews.

For cheap eats there are a number of good, clean, south Indian *thali* houses around the Municipal Gardens, all serving meals for around Rs20 per head.

Inland from Margao

Rachol Seminary: The College of The Good Shepherd

This grand old Jesuit institution and its adjacent ruined fort lie in Salcete *taluka*, five short miles northeast of town. The seminary has been constantly active since its inception in 1580, not ceasing its work and worship even after being sacked by Bijapuri raiders, nor following the expulsion of its Jesiut founders in the 1750s. The seminary (most of whose present structure was rebuilt in 1606) sits atop a hill just outside the village of **Raia**—a defensive position overlooking the river Zuari.

Rachol survived both the Maratha invasion of 1680–83 (when its now-derelict fort held the armies of mounted raiders at bay for months) and by the 18th century had become known as one of the prime seats of learning of the Catholic world: the seminary had a printing press installed the same year it was built, on which were printed the first Konkani-language Bibles, and in 1782 its church was deemed sufficiently important to receive some holy relics of St Constantine, the evangelical Byzantine emperor, a few of whose bones are said to be stuck in the altarpiece. There is plenty of gilded carving and the chancel is decorated with frescoes.

Rachol's most attractive feature is its central courtyard, surrounded by pillared walkways. Under the flagstones of the courtyard itself lies a huge water cistern—the seminary's old freshwater supply. Part of this courtyard was excavated earlier this century and a large, headless statue of a Nandi Bull (Shiva's animal 'vehicle') was discovered underneath, proving that the seminary occupies the site of a former Shiva temple—or perhaps a complex of temples, destroyed by the intolerant Catholics during the early years of colonial rule. You can also visit the seminary's great hall, hung with Renaissance portraits of Goa's high clergy—a brutish-looking lot, and some second-rate copies of portraits of the Portuguese royal families.

The nearby **ruined fort** was originally built by the Bijapuris in the 15th century, was added to by the Vijayanagars in the 16th century and taken over by the Portuguese in the 1580s. Only its gateway survives fully intact. The place has been derelict for over 150 years, but although today's hunks of fractured masonry give little clue of the fort's former impregnability, it was once Goa's main inland artillery centre. If you are going to explore it, beware of snakes among the rocks, particularly *kraits* and cobras—it is just their kind of habitat.

Safer to wander around is the curiously-named church of **Our Lady of the Snows** down on the Zuari river bank below the fort. The church is notable for the tombs of five Jesuits who were murdered by outraged Hindus during the 1570s— the height of the era of temple destruction.

Loutolim

Just west of the Raia–Ponda road lies the old village of **Loutolim**, which has perhaps the greatest concentration of colonial villas in the whole state, as well as a particularly lovely church with a three-storey white-washed Baroque façade and a tiled church tower tacked on the side. Just wandering around Loutolim's few dusty streets is lovely; red and purple bougainvillaea climbs up the sides of the handsome houses and over their wide, shady verandahs. The pitched red-tiled roofs and church-like arched windows are typical of the best of Goan colonial architecture. If you have a little time it is well worth visiting the grandest of all the village's houses, the **Miranda House**.

Roughly contemporary with the great villas of Margao, the Miranda House was built in the late 1600s but incorporates various later additions. It rises two storeys and owes more to European Baroque than Goan style, with some beautiful early wrought-ironwork along its upper balconies. Like the Margao houses, the Miranda House displays some very beautiful carved rosewood furniture and can be visited by prior arrangement with the tourist office in Margao, along with two other fine Loutolim villas, the **Roque Caetan House** (built 1815–20) and the **Salvador Costa House**. All are constructed around a central flower-filled courtyard. If you haven't the time to arrange to see the interiors before going out, it is still worth knocking on the door and asking to look round; if the owners feel that your interest is genuine and they have some free time, they are usually happy to oblige. You will be expected to make a donation of between Rs50 and Rs100 per head.

Loutolim also has a newly opened piece of eccentricity: a sort of museum complex called 'Ancestral Goa'. It is owned by the son of one of the local wealthy families, who recently came back from Art School and has carved a huge sculpture—apparently one of the largest in India—on one of the hillsides just out of the village. Hewn from the local laterite, it represents Mirra Bai, a female Hindu saint, playing on her veena. The sculpture is quite outrageous in its scale but the artist's other project, Ancestral Goa, is even more so. Occupying his old family villa and surrounding buildings, the complex consists of the old Portuguese house, a Malabar Hindu house, a reconstructed fisherman's cottage, a taverna, a cobbler, barber, feni distillery, spice garden and orchard. Entrance is Rs30 per head. To find Ancestral Goa, head for the main village church and ask someone for 'Bigfoot'. Apparently the sculptor and owner has carved a large dancing shoe near the entrance of his villa and the museum complex is locally known by this new landmark.

Chandor and the Pandava Caves

Another handsome colonial village, Chandor, lies about 4 miles east of Margao and like Loutolim has survived as a treasure-trove of colonial architecture. Its Jesuit church, **Our Lady of Bethlehem**, built in the 1640s but extensively restored at various times since then, is especially worth visiting in January, when the church has a big **festival**, the Feast of the Three Kings, on January 6. An informal, riotous affair that sharply contrasts with the sombre festival processions of Old Goa, this semi-pagan affair somehow more than any other encapsulates the spirit of Goa. Part medieval fair, part Indian religious frenzy with something of old Europe and much of timeless Asia, it centres around a procession of saints' effigies accompanied by white-robed ecclesiastics and devotees. The smell of incense, the crack of fireworks, complacent cows and reeling drunks, flirtatious Konkani and Lambadi tribal women with silver ingots in their hair and demure young Catholic girls in virgin white: the Feast of the Three Kings is worth seeing.

Chandor has another attraction that can be seen at any time of year: the **Menenzes Braganza House**. One of the largest villas in the state, this villa was home to the Indian Catholic journalist Luis de Menenzes Braganza, one of the leading lights of Goa's 19th-century independence movement, as well as to his grandsons, who formed the Goa National Congress in 1928. The family, originally high-caste Hindus, converted in the late 1600s but have lived in the villa since the 16th century. The interior is properly aristocratic rather than colonial, with a vast reception salon hung with crystal chandeliers and superb 18th-century furniture. There is a library of over 5000 books, mostly in Portuguese, but some in English and other European as well as Indian languages. The small Baroque chapel is still in use. The Menenzes Braganza family is still very wealthy, owning huge estates in Saclete *taluka*, and has the resources to maintain the house in its grand style. As with all the great Goan houses, you have to make a prior arrangement if you want to view it: contact the Tourist Office on Miranda Road in Margao, ✆ 222513.

Signposted from Chandor's main plaza is the ancient site of **Chandrapura**, the old Mauryan capital of Konkan (*see* **History**, p.34), as the Goan territory was known in the last centuries BC. Built by the great Mauryan Emperor Ashoka sometime in the 4th century BC, the site was continuously occupied through the early centuries AD, finally becoming a regional capital of the early medieval Chalukyan kings of the Deccan, who ruled the Konkan between the 6th and 10th centuries.

Excavated in 1929, the site of Chandrapura is still effectively just waste-ground covered with scrub woodland, and with no convenient little tourist-board signs tell you what was where. In fact, apart from a few bits of fallen masonry, long overgrown, you are more likely to notice the colourful bird-life, especially the green bee-eaters, black-headed orioles and parakeets that flicker among the sunlit trunks, than get any feeling of a great and faded past—there is little of Chandrapura left above the ground and the site has been abandoned since the 11th century.

About 12 miles southeast of Chandor, a short footpath leads from the village of **Rivona** through thick woods to a rock-cut Buddhist sanctuary known as the **Pandava Caves**. Built in the 7th century AD the sanctuary, like Chandrapura, is an unspectacular ruin and consists of monks' cells cut into a small cliff-face. Archaeologists think that the caves were hewn by hand by the monks who lived here.

Buddhists were often persecuted under the Chalukyan rule and this site was probably kept secret until its abandonment sometime in the 11th or 12th century. Later carvings depicting Hanuman and other deities in some of the caves indicate that the site was taken over by Hindus in the later medieval period, but today there is no working place of worship here.

Only two caves survive: a large worship chamber with a dais at one end and a smaller living cell. The original site probably included other structures built of boulders, but these have long since disappeared. Casual travellers may find Rivona rather unexciting. As with Goa's only other (and even plainer) Buddhist sanctuary at Arvalem in Bicholim *taluka* to the north, the Pandava caves are worth knowing about, but only history buffs will feel them to be worth making a special effort to visit.

Ponda's Temple Villages

A rural hinterland of rice paddies, spice plantations and wooded valleys, Ponda makes a tranquil contrast with the busier coast. Its sleepy villages have a palpable langour, being as yet unmotivated by the desire to make money from tourism, for tourists only visit a small part of the *taluka*. Those who do come stick to a small area around Ponda, the regional town whose surrounding villages have some superb Hindu temples. These make an easy day trip from the coast. However, if you can spare the time it is worth spending a couple of days exploring Ponda *taluka*. The countryside is very pretty and to the east rise the steep foothills of the Western Ghats, which can be explored via the Bondla Wildlife Sanctuary (*see* p. 118).

NB: Visitors to Hindu temples must remove their shoes before entering.

History

Ponda *taluka* begins just 3 miles east of Old Goa, yet it was not brought under Portuguese rule until the late 18th century (1762) after the Inquisition had been abolished. Ponda's villages had been havens for idols saved from the coastal temples when they were destroyed by the Portuguese in the 16th and 17th centuries. The idols were smuggled down the Mandovi or across the Zuari Rivers to be hidden in secret shrines in Ponda's forested valleys, and while the local Hindu rulers were careful not to openly encourage this flouting of their Catholic neighbours' religious strictures, their 'open door' policy made sure that Hinduism in Goa was never stamped out. Once the Inquisition had been abolished in the 1750s Ponda's rulers built new temples to house these old idols. A whole rash of temple complexes were put up around the town of Ponda, at a respectable distance from the original Portuguese territory. Funds for their upkeep were granted in perpetuity, and the temples are still maintained to a high standard.

Temple Styles

The temples of Ponda are unique in their architecture, being the only Hindu structures in India to borrow directly from Portuguese Baroque. They are faintly European in feel, with pilastres and vaulted roofs, topped by domed 'church' towers. Many of the temples also have free-standing lamp towers next to them. These tall whitewashed structures have tier upon tier of alcoves in which oil lamps are lit on festival nights, creating magical pillars of light. The lamp towers are thought to have been brought by the Marathas who invaded eastern Goa during the late 17th century. But while a few lamp towers do occur in present-day Maharashtra, these days the design is more or less confined to Goa.

The Temples

The easiest way to get to the temples is to take the road east from Old Goa to **Banastari**, a village, and then continue a further six miles towards Ponda. The temples can be found in several villages about one mile before you reach the town. Most are signposted from the road. The temple villages are: **Mardol**, **Priol**, **Velinga**, **Farmagudi**, **Queula** and **Bandola**.

Getting Around

While you can see some of Ponda's temples on official tours (*see* **Travel**, p.15) it is far more relaxing to wander around them at your own leisure. You can reach them either by bus (services to Ponda run about once every half-hour from Panjim and Margao), or you can hire a taxi and driver to take you. If you do hire a driver, don't pay more than Rs200 per person for the round trip from Panjim. From Margao don't pay more than Rs300 per person.

The first temple on the way east from Panjim is the **Shri Mangesh Temple** at Priol. A Shiva temple, it was built in the 18th century to house an ancient (probably early medieval) lingam that had been rescued from a temple near Cortalim following its destruction by the Inquisition in the early 1600s.

Shri Mangesh is a large temple, brightly painted and spick and span inside and out. Its design includes several European features, most notably the false pillars with Doric capitals lining the outside walls, which are painted a jolly yellow. This European influence contrasts with the eastern-style whitewashed porch, roof and lamp tower, which stands just to the side of the temple.

About half a mile further on, just before Mardol, is the **Shri Mahalsa Temple**. Its history is remarkably similar to that of Shri Mangesh—it was built in the mid-1700s to house a sacred idol from Cortalim, this time of Mahalsa, which can be interpreted both as a female aspect of Vishnu or as a spiritual aspect of Lakshmi, the goddess of wealth; Lakshmi is Vishnu's wife (at least, when he's in his ordinary avatar or incarnation). How confusing Hinduism is.

The Shri Mahalsa temple is more attractive than Shri Mangesh, being traditionally designed in the Malabar style: steeply pitched, red-tiled roofs all interconnecting and overhanging low to shady porches held up by carved hardwood columns. The carving continues inside, in a frieze depicting the 10 avatars of Vishnu.

Another mile further south brings you to Velinga village and its **Shri Lakshmi Narasimha Temple**, another 18th-century affair, though smaller than the temples at Priol and Mardol. Again, the European style is evident in pillars and Baroque motifs. Lakshmi Narasimha poses another set of interpretive problems: Narasimha is the half-man, half-lion aspect of Vishnu, the last and highest of his several animal avatars, which he adopted in his progression from basic creation to his more divine forms, while Lakshmi is his wife. Quite why the two should be worshipped as one is unclear, and the author could not find a priest to explain it properly.

About three miles southwest of Velinga is Bandola village, where there are several temples. Largest is the **Shri Nangesh Temple**, yet another 18th-century construction, occupying the site of an older temple, testified to by the survival of its carved foundation stone (dated 1413) in the wall of the temple tank outside. Again, there are fine wood carvings to see, this time depicting episodes from the sacred Sanskrit writings *Ramayana* and *Mahabharata*, religious epics that can be traced back several thousand years. Nangesh is a peaceful aspect of Shiva and the temple has a very phallic lingam that is topped with a carved face.

A short walk away is the **Shri Mahalaxshmi Temple**, another 18th-century temple built on the site of a 15th-century one. Yet again, the precise object of the temple's worship is complicated. Although Mahalaxshmi is a greater form of Lakshmi, the goddess of wealth and wife of Vishnu, in this temple she is represented as a female aspect of Shiva, the idol having a lingam carved into her hair. Again, this is confusing as Lakshmi is more generally regarded as a female aspect of Vishnu, her husband. Quite how she has come to be an aspect of Shiva here is unclear, unless one assumes that Shiva, being the creator *is* in fact all the other gods and goddesses, or rather they are him. There are so many differing cults and philosphies within Hinduism that one can never clear up such questions neatly. What *is* known is that the idol was smuggled out of Colva from the ruins of its original temple in 1565 and hidden in the forest nearby for 200 years until the present temple was built. Despite its theological complexity, the Shri Mahalaxshmi is only a small building and does not have a lamp tower.

From Bandola head back towards Farmagudi village, just north of Ponda town, and take the signpost for Queula village. After a short walk you will come to the impressive **Shri Shantadurga Temple**, built in 1738. The title Shantadurga offers a clue to the type of worship of this particular temple: 'shanta' means peace and 'Durga' was one of the names for Shiva's wife (or his female aspect if you prefer), who is known by several titles, each one indicating a different aspect. Durga is a goddess of peace or at least a peacemaker. Riding a lion, she brought harmony to the firmament for a while by slaying a particularly troublesome buffalo-headed demon called Durga. The goddess then took his name as a kind of trophy. Later on she proved her abilities a second time by settling a quarrel between Shiva and Vishnu that was threatening to blow the universe apart. She has the power to dispel all negativity and false perception.

This temple sees a lot of pilgrims who come to ask special favours from the goddess—often to do with settling disputes—or to give thanks for a deliverance from danger. Again, the idol is an early medieval one that was smuggled into Ponda during the late 1500s. Occasionally the idol is brought out and paraded through the village in a giant wooden temple chariot drawn by hundreds of young devotees. The chariots or temple cars are housed in a kind of hangar behind the temple and are worth seeing for the contrast of their intricate carvings and giant scale of construction. Opposite the Shantadurga is a small temple of similar age, dedicated to Lord Ramnath (Rama) the divine warrior and protector—one of Vishnu's higher avatars.

If you decide to overnight in Ponda *taluka*, head from Bondola village into Ponda town, just a couple of short miles away and book into one of the hotels or guesthouses here before moving on to the mountain forests or the spice plantations of the steep hill country further east.

Ponda Town

Incorporated into Portuguese Goa in 1791, Ponda is a small agricultural town that services the surrounding farm country. It is a sleepy place and typifies the deep langour of Goa's smaller country towns. Some handsome old villas lining the streets and a ruined fort give the place a period atmosphere.

moderate

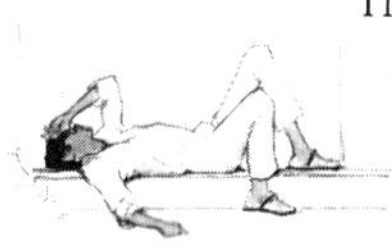

The **Hotel Atish**, © 32239 or 32439, is just north of Ponda in the small hamlet of Farmagudi. It has comfortable rooms, some with air-conditioning and a restaurant serving both Goan and south Indian vegetarian food.

inexpensive

The **Hotel Kirti**, © 32801, is in the centre of Ponda on Nirankal Road. It has fairly basic but clean rooms with fans, as does the **Hotel Pearl**, © 32141 or 32243, on Main Road.

cheap

Ponda's only non-flea-ridden cheap lodges are **Julie's Inn**, © 222566, near the Municipal Building, or the **Central Tourist Home** in the Parvati Building. Both are situated just off Main Road in the small town centre.

The Safa Shahouri Mosque

he only grand medieval mosque left standing by the Portuguese, Safa Shahouri is ust a short (10-minute) motorbike-taxi ride northeast of Ponda. It was built in 560 by the Adil Shah of Bijapur (*see* **History**, p.36), constructed of local red latrite but whitewashed against the sun's heat. The mosque is small and elegant, vith a pitched Goan roof rather than the more usual Muslim dome—a necessary racticality given the violence of Goa's monsoon storms. The walls are decorated vith tall arches in the wide, pointed Bijapuri style. The bases of long-fallen pillars how that there was once a large outer forecourt. Some partly ruined steps lead lown to a temple tank.

Spice Plantations and Wild Forests

s you travel further north of Ponda town, the landscape of paddies gives way to nes of spice shrubs, mostly cardamom, shaded by tall hardwood trees, climbed y twisting vines of wild pepper. Some of these plantations can be visited; visit the anjim tourist office for details.

f you travel 10 miles east of Ponda town, passing through the village of Usgao, locks of hardwood forest gradually begin to take over and spurs of the Western hat mountains snake down from the blue ranges in the far east of the *taluka*.

You can get into the forests for **trekking** and **wildlife viewing** at **Bondla Wildlife Sanctuary** just south of Usgao. Bondla has a sort of open zoo of indigenous wildlife as well as a great sweep of wild country behind that is home to most of the south Indian species. Full details of Bondla and Goa's other wild areas are given in the chapter on wildlife sanctuaries, *see* pp 117–120.

Gaur

Goa's Wildlife Sanctuaries

After the initial look of panic, the bull regains its composure. He stands there for what must be a minute—then with a toss of his head and a grunt of alarm he turns away from you. As if by magic the grass seems to explode as bison struggle to their feet. The bull leads them out of the glade into the jungle and soon they are gone.

Kunal Verma, *The Bison*

Few travellers to Goa manage to prise themselves from the beaches and explore the nearby mountains. But those who do will discover an accessible wilderness of dry deciduous forests, small rainforests, waterfalls, river gorges and wildlife sanctuaries. There is good **trekking** in the sanctuaries, most of which are within two hours of the beach, and the forests are still well populated with wildlife.

The World Wide Fund for Nature (WWF) is particularly active in Goa and the conservation movement here has more influence with the government than in many other Indian states. The Goan branch of the WWF is based in Panjim and offers guided treks into the mountains. Although you can travel independently into most of the wild areas, going with a guide will increase your chances of seeing animals. The guide will also explain the local ecosystem and can usually identify the flora. For more information contact the **WWF Goan Divisional Office**, Hillside Apartments, Block B, B-2, Ground Floor, Fontainas (off 31 January Street), Panjim, Goa 403001, ✆ (0832) 226020. Another worthwhile contact is the **Hiking Association of Goa**, located at 6 Anand Niwas, Captain of Port's Office, Vivekanda Road, Panjim, ✆ (0832) 5070. However, while this organisation can get you into wild areas, it will often be in a noisy group, which is fun socially, but tends to scare off the wildlife.

If you want to arrange trekking before you go, contact Ranjan Abraham at **Clipper Holidays**, Suite 406, Regency Enclave, 4 Magrath Road, Bangalore 560 025, ✆/📠 (080) 5599032/34/5599833, tlx 0845-3095. He can arrange accommodation, equipment and guides without you needing to run around when you get there.

Bondla Wildlife Sanctuary

This is Goa's smallest sanctuary at only 3 square miles and is 30 miles east of Panjim at Ponda Takula. You can reach it by bus from Panjim (2 hours) via Ponda, and there are regular hourly services between the city and the sanctuary.

Bondla is more of a zoological park than a wild reserve—although the surrounding conserved forest is very wild, it is possible to **trek** into the wilderness via the WWF in Panjim (*see* above). Indigenous wildlife is kept in large, open-air fenced areas. Of particular note are the semi-domesticated herds of *gaur* (bison), who come very close to the fence and offer superb possibilities for photography. In the surrounding

Chital

forest, the largest animals are a migratory herd of wild elephant who come in from Karnataka during the dry season (February–August). Trekking during these months can thus be dangerous and should not be attempted without a guide. Other local wildlife includes leopard, sloth bear, *sambar* and *chital* (spotted) deer, wild boar and common *langur* monkey. A few hundred yards into the forest from the reception office is a waterhole overlooked by a large *machan* or viewing platform, built into a tree. Again, this offers good chances for photography, but it can also make a good place to spend the night if you can persuade the local Wildlife Department officials. You will need a mosquito net for protection against insects and snakes. There is more comfortable accommodation in a Forest Department resthouse but this is usually booked up by school groups. If you want to stay overnight, bring a tent or mosquito net and ask the people at the reception office to let you pitch it somewhere quiet—they are usually amenable.

Bird species at Bondla include paradise flycatcher, racket-tail drongo, grey hornbill and peacock.

Bhagwan Mahavir Wildlife Sanctuary

About 35 miles east of Panjim near the village of Sanguem Taluka, this is a much larger sanctuary than nearby Bondla (about 90 square miles). The dense forest harbours similar game species to Bondla, and there is **trekking** down to the **Dudhsagar Waterfalls** and to the deep **Devil's Canyon**. You can reach the sanctuary by bus from Panjim (journey time about 3 hours, services run every 1½ hours).

The waterfalls can also be reached by a light-gauge **railway** that runs from Margao (journey time about 4 hours, services 3 times daily) and can be treated as a day trip from the southern beaches.

Accommodation at Bhagwan Mahavir is in two Forest Department resthouses. There is generally room if you *insist* on staying, although the Wildlife Department officials at the reception office often claim that the resthouses are full. As with most of the Goan sanctuaries, your best bet of getting in is via a WWF trip (*see* above).

Langur

Birds are also the same as for Bondla, with the addition of Malabar trogon, great pied hornbill, ruby-throated yellow bulbul (wow!) and the magnificent crested serpent eagle.

Cotigao Wildlife Sanctuary

This is another large conservation area—about 40 square miles—but in the far south of the state. The easiest way to reach Cotigao is by bus from Canacona, near Palolem (services every hour, journey time about an hour) and there is accommodation in one small resthouse. However, it is very difficult to get permission to stay here. If you want to get into Cotigao, you are more or less on your own. You will need a tent and a good compass, as no maps or guides are available. Camping in the forest is safe as there are no elephants or tigers but getting lost is a real problem. The dense undergrowth has innumerable narrow paths snaking through it, trodden by local tribals gathering wood and these form an immense labyrinth. Again, unless you are a very experienced hiker and have all your own food, it is best to arrange a trip through the WWF in Panjim (*see* above).

Again, the fauna is the same as for Bondla and Bhagwan Mahavir sanctuaries. Bird-watchers should look out for the white-eyed buzzard eagle, rufous woodpecker, the Malabar crested lark and rosy minivet.

Other Conserved Areas of Goa

Goa has about 5000 acres of mangrove swamp around its river estuaries. The largest areas are along the Zuari river delta, the Mandovi river delta, along the Cumbarjua canal and at a few spots near Chapora and Terekol in the northern beaches. There has even been some re-planting of destroyed mangroves. About four million seedlings have been planted since 1985 but the success rate has been low (under 50 per cent). For the most part, it is impossible to explore these swamps—not only are they physically difficult to enter without a boat, but permission for entry is officially denied as the government wants the areas left undisturbed.

However, there are two bird sanctuaries where tourists can see the swamps. Two miles outside Panjim on the road to Old Goa is the **Chorao Bird Sanctuary** which covers about 500 acres. Its mangrove-fringed mud flats attract thousands of migratory birds and provide excellent bird-watching, especially from November to March. Among the migrants that fly in during these months are huge flocks of sandpipers, stilts and snipe, pin-tail ducks, shoveler ducks, purple moorhens, several species of tern, adjutant storks, teal and garganey.

Seven miles from Panjim at Carambolim is another sanctuary, **Karmali Lake**. At about 140 acres, Karmali also has a November–February season. The migratory bird species are the same as for Chorao sanctuary but with the addition of lesser whistling teal, whitenecked storks and *nakta* (combduck). Year-round residents include dabchicks, night and reef herons, bitterns, brahmini duck, glossy ibis, open-bill stork, kites and marsh harrier. There are regular buses from Panjim to Carambolim but from there you will have to take an auto-rickshaw or taxi.

The Karnataka and Kerala Beaches

It was just about noon, and far away, high above even the tallest trees, a fish-hawk called its shrill, long cry. Trilling down the lonely paths of the blue sky, radiant with the midday brilliance of the autumn sun, it was like the voice of a goddess.

Bhibhutibushan Banerji, *Pather Panchali,*
or *The Song of the Road*

Goa is not the only part of the Malabar Coast with beautiful beaches. Just to the south in Karnataka state, the coast is just being discovered by travellers and, although conditions are very basic, you can find the solitude (and cheap prices) that Goa used to have back in the hippy days of the 1970s. South of Karnataka, in Kerala state, the beaches are a little more developed, but the development is still on a much lower scale than in Goa and again prices are cheaper, except in the private resort hotels of the far south.

Getting There

The beaches of **Karnataka** can all be reached by bus within a few hours from southern Goa. For **Kerala**, you should travel by bus as far as Mangalore, then take a train or bus south. Bekal beach is about 3 hours' bus ride from Mangalore, while the southern beaches are a further 10–12 hours away, via the state capital Trivandrum.

Karnataka

Most Karnataka beaches are for the adventurous traveller only, having no facilities of any kind. However, at Karwar and Gokarn you can now find basic comfort, and the beaches—especially those at Gokarn—are perhaps the most beautiful on the whole of the Malabar Coast.

Karwar

Karwar lies 20 miles south of the Goan border and about 2 hours by bus from Margao. Although an ugly town, it has useful facilities such as banks—all the long-stay travellers from the Gokarn beaches further south come up here to change money. You can find quiet, little-used beaches 20 minutes' walk from town; not quite as picturesque as those at Gokarn but then there are fewer travellers and, as yet, no facilities beyond *chai*-shops, so you have to camp.

The town has several cheap lodges where you can leave your belongings before heading for the beaches. Try the **Anand Bhavan**, which has doubles for under Rs100 with attached bucket bathroom and Indian toilet. If the Anand is full the **Hotel Ashok**, by the bus station, or the **Govardhan** are good value and reasonably clean, but you will need a mosquito net.

Gokarn

Gokarn (situated another hour south of Karwar by bus) is a jewel—an unspoilt town of old Keralan-style houses with wooden-slatted balconies rising to several stories. The streets radiate out from an ancient sanskrit school and college for brahmins. There are several medieval temples, and two huge temple cars stand in the main street, which is lined with stalls selling religious accoutrements for trainee priests—images of gods, incense holders, brass bells, pestle and mortars and holy pictures. The brahmins, heads shaven but for the top-knot that signifies their office, bustle to and fro in white lungis, caste cords lying diagonally across their bare chests. The young brahmins are wiry, underfed and obsequious; their seniors often obscenly fat. All are full of quiet disdain for scruffy Western backpackers.

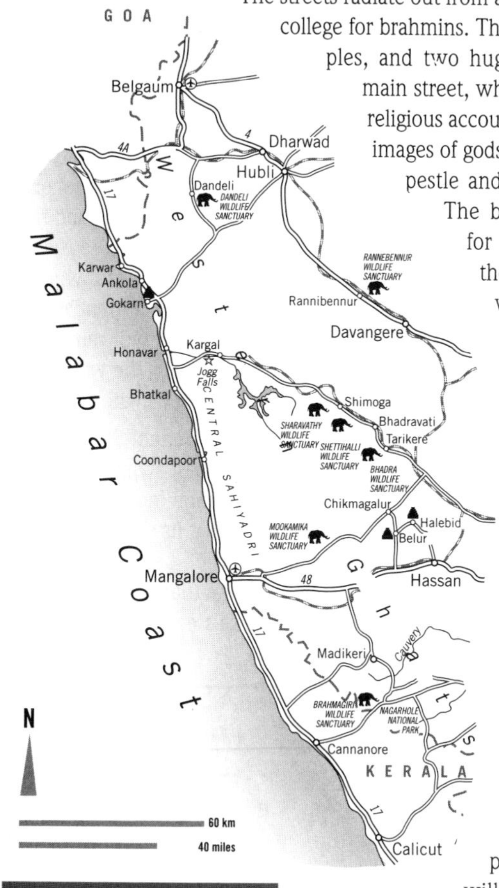

Despite the architectural beauty of the town, it is Gokarn's wonderful scimitar-shaped **beaches** that most attracts the traveller. You should allow at least a week to enjoy them properly. Once you have made the trip along the rocky path down to the sea, you will not want to get back on a loud, sweaty bus for some time.

The Karnataka Coast

Gokarn's Beaches

Avoid Gokarn's town beach (except for a walk when you first arrive) and check into one of the lodges for the night. Take the small alley that leads away between small houses to the left of the big temple car shed as you walk down from the bus stand. The alley soon emerges from the houses and becomes a path that snakes uphill over black and pink volcanic rocks to **Kudle Beach**, the closest piece of paradise to the town. This walk takes about half an hour and should be done in the early morning or evening, before or after the main heat of the day. You can leave the bulk of your gear under lock and key at one of the lodges in Gokarn and just take the bare necessities over to the beaches (the first two also have safe places to leave clothes and money). If the sun does get too hot on your walk, you can stop at a small *chai*-shop, appropriately called the **Halfway House**, and drink sodas in the shade until the sun loses its ferocity.

Kudle Beach is, like all the beaches of Gokarn, a long, curved strip of white and gold sand set between two forested headlands. A strip of paddies and coconut palms occupies a narrow flat strip inland from the beach. After this the ground rises steeply to the first foothills of the Western Ghats, which tumble almost to the sea on this part of the Malabar Coast. Because Kudle Beach is the closest to town, it is the most 'developed', but this only means it has three timber-and-thatch *chai*-houses serving food and drink. For next-to-nothing these places will rent you a palm-thatch or *adobe* hut to stash your gear in while you swim in the warm, lapping ocean, drink *chai*, eat fish or *thalis* and sleep on the beach by night.

A half-hour's walk on from Kudle, over the headland, is **Om Beach**. Smaller than Kudle, the water here is calmer and offers some of Gokarn's best swimming. Tranquil, and a good place to see dolphins, the beach gets its name not from stoned hippies chanting on its sands, but from the locals, who say that its shape resembles that of the sacred Om if seen from the hills above. The beach has one tea-house serving food, but no organized place to stay. A couple of palm-thatch beach shelters serve as wind-breaks if you want to sleep here. The locals are prone to stealing anything left unguarded, however, so keep your valuables within sight at all times.

One more half-hour walk southward over the next headland takes you to **Half-Moon Beach**. Here there is not a single *chai*-house, and it makes a great place to camp. But food and water are problems: there is no natural spring as at Kudle and Om and so you'll have to go back to Om for your sustenance unless you have the foresight to bring your own supplies.

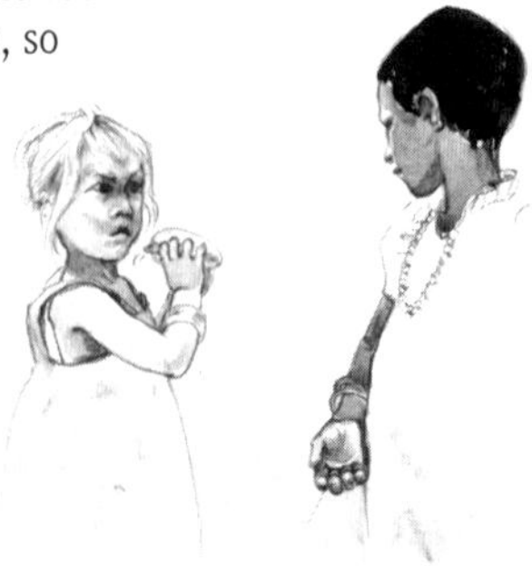

A final half-hour's southward hike over a last wooded headland and you are on **Paradise Beach**, so called for its near-inaccessibility and complete peace—nothing but the sea, the sky, the sand and you. Unfortunately, there is no fresh-water supply here either but this does not stop people from hiking in and losing themselves for weeks.

One word of warning: recently reports of night-time muggings have come in from people staying out at Half-Moon and Paradise Beaches. The classic scenario seems to be local toughs either demanding money from women walking alone on one of the headlands, or attacking lone travellers and couples sleeping on the beach. The best way to avoid this is to get together with some others when sleeping. If this is not possible, head back to Kudle or Om before dark, where there will always be a few other travellers, and sleep there.

Where to Stay

Gokarn Town © (08386–)

Gokarn's most expensive hotel, **Om Lodge**, © 4644/4645/46244, is not the best place to stay, but it has the most modern-style rooms (some with air-conditioning). It tends to fill up with large groups of Indian tourists come to worship at the town's temples and its food is not of the highest standard. Rooms are clean, however (inexpensive).

Gokarn has several very cheap guest lodges, all clustered together about half a mile from the bus stand on the main street. Walk up the way the bus is pointing, then turn left at the T-junction and keep walking for about 3 minutes and you will come to a few lodges. However, only one warrants recommendation, the **Vaibhav Nivas Lodge**, © 46289 (cheap) set back a little from the road. Run by a family of Brahmins, this has double rooms with shower and (Indian) toilet attached, or cheaper ones with shared bathrooms. The lodge occupies an old Karnatik house and there are pet birds (and two white rats) in cages, reasonable food, and beer for sale. The Vaibhav will look after your belongings for Rs5 per day.

Beaches

The only place resembling an organized lodge is the *chai*-shop at the foot of the headland path as it comes down to Kudle beach. Here you can eat and rent a secure *adobe* hut (with padlock) to sleep in or stash your rucksacks. There is a 'shower' consisting of a hose attached to the local freshwater spring. If this place is full, which is unlikely, the owners will direct you to one or two other places on the beach where you can sleep and leave your gear but in slightly less secure palm-thatch huts. On the other beaches you have to camp in the open.

Eating Out

Gokarn Town

You can eat at the cheap restaurant in the **Om Lodge** and drink beer with the local drunks. To do the same but with other travellers try the **Vaibhav Nivas Lodge** (*see* above). On the same road as the cheap lodges you can find some very good, cheap *thali*-houses.

Beaches

Kudle Beach has two places to eat: a sort of guest lodge at the foot of the headland path leading back to town, which serves indifferent *thalis* and fish, or the really good but unnamed restaurant, set among some kept gardens just back from the centre of the beach and owned by a Spanish lady who came to stay for a while and ended up marrying a local. Her restaurant serves home-made garlicky pasta (oh joy!) and fish. She also has a charming dalmation dog. Prices are very cheap.

At Om Beach there is another *chai*-shop serving *thalis*, *parathas* and some Western food (cheese on toast, omelettes, etc). Again, prices are very cheap.

Kerala

For a long time the haunt only of hippies and travellers looking for a quiet backwater away from the teeming bustle of Northern India, Kerala's coast has now been officially 'discovered' and the old hippy beaches of **Kovalam** and **Varkala** are fast becoming developed for mass tourism. But as ever in traveller's India, the demise of one place's tranquility coincides with the discovery of somewhere new: in this case the (as yet) undeveloped cove at **Bekal** on Kerala's northern coast, where the only accommodation is in an old fort and the visitor can share the beach with local fishermen and few others.

Bekal

About 3 hours south of Mangalore by bus, Bekal is what Kovalam and Varkala were until a few years ago: secluded, visited by only a few 'real' travellers, dirt cheap, quiet, with clean beaches and good swimming. There is also an interesting fort where you can stay. The fort dates from the early medieval period and has some superb airy interiors, yet, having been taken over as a state-run guest house, it costs only about Rs100 per night (less if you bargain).

Varkala

Varkala beach is reached from the town of Quilon, exactly 1 hour by train from Trivandrum (30 miles; several services daily). A delightful, unspoilt little resort, Varkala has a mineral-water spring, a Vishnu temple dedicated to Lord Janardhana with fascinating rituals, a beach that is empty except at weekends, good swimming and lovely country scenery.

The Kerala Coast

Apart from a minor problem with theft, the beach and its small village are mercifully free from the hassle of Kovalam to the south—no groups of Indian tourists turning out to see European flesh and few hawkers. Visit soon however, as Varkala's beauty has not gone unnoticed; the Taj hotel group is planning to build a huge resort hotel and golf course on the cliffs above the beach.

Where to Stay

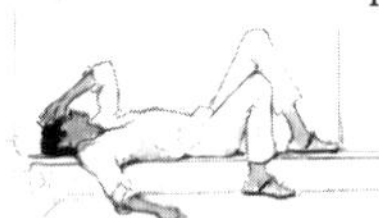

The more expensive places to stay are in the 'moderate' price category. They include the **Hill Top Beach Resort** and the **Varkala Marine Palace**—both with prices starting at Rs300 per person, but it is better to eschew these rather bland places and head for the cheaper, friendlier lodges nearer the beach. For Rs100 or less for a double try the **Tourist Home**, the **Mamma Home** in an old Keralan house and the ambitiously named but very basic **Beach Palace**. Long-stay travellers can find rooms in local houses for about Rs35 per night. Some travellers book into the cheap lodges in the town itself, mainly in the area of the Krishna temple: a famous saint called Sri Narayana used to live here and many followers have stayed on.

Kovalam

Kovalam, 7 miles south of Trivandrum (and connected by half-hourly bus services), was once the Arabian Sea beach resort of the court of the Rajahs of Travancore. Today, its two scimitar-sweeps of sand comprise the most popular tourist draw in southern Kerala. The place used only to cater for hippy backpackers but now matches Goa for restaurants, hotels and shopping. However, despite a massive increase in visitors Kovalam still has its soft yellow-white sands, warm, clear waters and wide views of the ocean horizon. Small beach restaurants provide the laid-back tourist community with fresh seafood and slightly overpriced Western-style cuisine.

Tourist Information

The nearest **tourist office** is in Trivandrum. So is **Indian Airlines**, the **State Bank of India** and the **post office**. To **change money** use the bank at **Kovalam Ashok Beach Resort**. To post letters, buy aerogrammes and the like use the small **sub post office** in Kovalam Village (a 20-minute climb up the back of the beach, near the top of the headland).

The Beaches

Kovalam has two popular beaches, separated by a large rock outcrop extending into the sea. The luxury beach, overlooked by the five-star Ashok Beach Resort Hotel, is just below the bus stand. The main beach with all the budget accommodation and beach restaurants is a 1-minute walk through shady palm groves from the bus stand. The end of this 'budget' beach is marked by the lighthouse up on the headland.

Popular beach activities at Kovalam include snorkelling (easy to hire equipment), water-skiing (contact the Ashok Hotel) and body-surfing the big waves about 200 yards off the shore. Swimming is very pleasant in the shallows, which extend a long way out, but don't go much further as the currents become dangerously strong.

Massage

Kovalam is full of places offering Ayurvedic massage, but of course there are also many charlatans. Head straight for **Medicus Massage** opposite the Rockholm Hotel on the Lighthouse road, a small clinic run by a husband and wife team, Drs K.R.C. and Lalitha Babu.

Kovalam ✆ (0471–)

Where to Stay

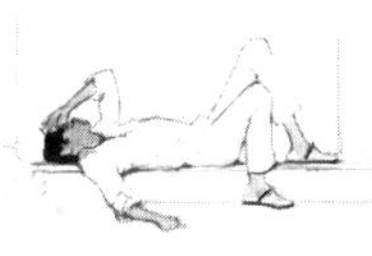

Note: In all of Kovalam's hotels you may be able to bargain discounts of up to 50% in the low season (any time apart from November to February).

luxury

The prestige place to stay is the five-star **Kovalam Ashok Beach Resort**, ✆ 68010/653236, @ 62522, with its superb location, watersports, yoga and massage facilities but the standard of service and food fluctuates. The beach cottages are pleasant but, as the air-conditioning rarely works, are not recommended in the hotter months. The large balcony rooms, which cost 25% higher between mid-December and the end of February, have the famous sunset view. A new wing opened in late 1992 and the old Palace guest house on the hill above the resort has four suites.

expensive

Try the well-appointed **Hotel Rockholm**, ✆ 584306, up on the lighthouse headland. This has some lovely, breezy rooms overlooking the cliffs and an excellent restaurant with open-air patio. KTDC's pleasant **Hotel Samudra**, ✆ 62089, a 15-minute walk north of the luxury Ashok hotel, is a modern building, tastefully done, commanding a quiet stretch of beach.

In season it has a good restaurant on the roof. Some rooms have balconies and sea views. You can also try the **Hotel Aparna** on Lighthouse Road, ✆ 64129/74367, which has rooms, again with some overlooking the sea.

moderate/inexpensive

Two hotels have rooms that fall within both categories. Directly behind the Rockholm on Lighthouse Road is **Syama Lodge** with huge, well-furnished rooms which drop to half-price in the low season. You can try for a big double room with a sea-view balcony at **Hotel Seaweed**, near the lighthouse, ✆ 480391.

cheap

There are now so many small, cheap and generally comfortable lodges, either right on the beach or set just back from it that recommending any one over another is a difficult exercise: they're changing all the time. Many have rooms from Rs100 per night and it is also possible to rent rooms with local families for Rs300 a week. Try the **Achuta Lodge Guest House**, the **Neptune Hotel** or **Holiday Home Guest House**—all on Lighthouse beach—or ask at any of the beach restaurants and you will soon find your way.

Eating Out

Kovalam has some excellent restaurants, although some of the old favourites on the beach have been closed down. Good Italian, French, Chinese and Malabar dishes plus the local seafood are all just a short, lazy stroll up the beach. Two popular beach restaurants are the **Black Cat** and **Coral**. The **Rockholm**, ✆ 306, has excellent fish dishes, depending on what's available that morning in the market. While the menu includes some European dishes it is their seafood that excels. Lobster, crab and mackerel can be prepared to order. Meals cost anything from Rs60–250 a head depending on how many dishes of crab curry you can eat. The **Searock** restaurant has a menu of Indian and continental dishes and meals are from about Rs60. No restaurant is in a hurry to serve you in Kovalam.

South of Kovalam

For those who can afford it there are several private beach resorts offering complete tranquility, a small number of guests at any time and hassle-free beaches shared only with the fishermen who go out at dawn and return at dusk. The closest to Kovalam (3 miles to the south) is **Lagoona Beach**, run by Kerala Tourism, ✆ 443738.

Occupying the meeting of several palm-fringed backwaters with the sea, this long sweep of empty beach is a perfect place to relax. Backwater trips to quiet villages are offered. Prices start from about Rs600 per person per night.

Much more expensive and much more exclusive is the **Surya Samudra Beach Garden** at Pulinkudi, some 5 miles further south, ✆ 480413/481824/481825, 📠 481124. Set in a sloping woodland of coconut palms, Surya Samudra (which means 'sun and sea' in Mallayalam) offers accommodation for just 24 people in antique, carved wood Keralan houses (imported from upcountry), two secluded beaches, a freshwater pool, one of the best restaurants in the state and landscaped grounds filled with ancient sculpture. Klaus, the German owner, has gradually developed the place from a single original house that he used to use as a private getaway while working as a teacher in Madras. He does his best to employ as many locals as possible, spends large amounts on local conservation and charges each guest a dollar a day for donation to the local villagers.

Best of all, Surya Samudra has Raju, one of Kerala's most gifted Ayurvedic doctors and masseurs. An hour and a half under his hands leaves you about a year younger. Raju is also a Kalaripayat martial arts master and his local school gives displays at the resort by request. Prices at Surya Samudra are very high: from Rs2000 per person per night.

A few miles south is the **Sometheeram Beach Resort**, ✆ 480600, 📠 481600. Designed along the same lines as Surya Samudra, with antique Keralan houses, an Ayurvedic spa and day trips to local sights, it lacks the former's intimacy. Prices are slightly lower though.

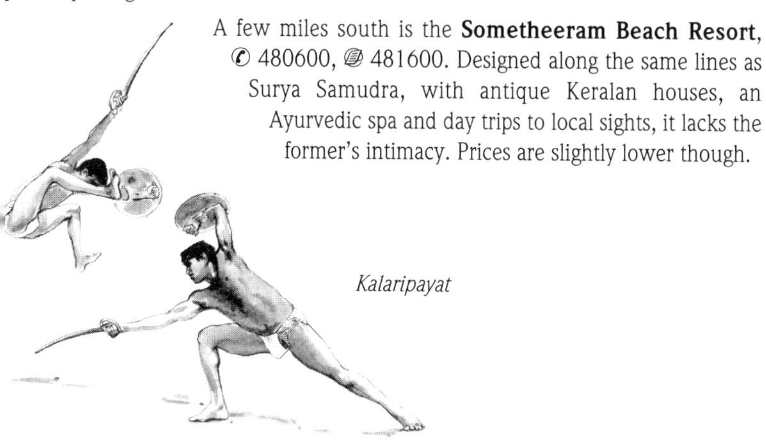

Kalaripayat

Main references are in **bold** type; page numbers of maps are in *italics*.

Index